BEYOND THE SHELTER WALL

Homeless Families Speak Out

ALSO BY RALPH DA COSTA NUNEZ

A Shelter is Not a Home... Or Is It?
The American Family Inn Handbook: A How-To Guide
The New Poverty: Homeless Families in America
Hopes, Dreams, & Promise: The Future of Homeless Children in America
Saily's Journey
Cooper's Tale
Our Wish

BEYOND THE SHELTER WALL

Homeless Families Speak Out

Ralph da Costa Nunez
President of Homes for the Homeless

– with –
Naomi Sugie

Foreword by
Leonard N. Stern
Founder of Homes for the Homeless

WHITE TIGER PRESS ◆ NEW YORK

Library of Congress Cataloging-in-Publication Data

Cover photography and design: © James E. Farnum

ISBN 0-9724425-1-0

© 2004 Homes for the Homeless, Inc.
White Tiger Press
32A Cooper Square, New York, NY 10003

212-529-5252

www.whitetigerpress.com

A White Tiger Book

Printed in the United States of America

For the mothers and children who gave their time,
told their stories, and let us listen.
Thank you.

CONTENTS

FOREWORD

I first met a homeless family nearly two decades ago, and since that time, I have heard the stories of hundreds. I have listened to teenage mothers—still children themselves—describe moving between relatives' homes with babies in tow until they exhausted all welcomes. I have heard stories of violence and abuse, of mothers and children escaping dangerous situations only to end up in homeless shelters. Most of all, I have heard stories of isolation, misfortune, and repeated mistakes.

It was sobering to learn why families became homeless and how a mother's current situation could be traced back to childhood. As I watched their children—young girls, boys, toddlers and babies—experiencing even greater upheaval, I felt the absolute need to reach out and help. Soon after my first visit to a shelter, I decided to start Homes for the Homeless to provide families with the assistance and guidance needed to better help them find their way. Since 1986, we have served over 24,000 families and 48,000 children, providing safe shelter, clean facilities, and enriching programs.

So many young mothers come to our doors lacking basic skills and direction in life. But within months, they earn high school diplomas, become job-ready, find daycare, regain a sense of control, and learn to better care for themselves and their children. While not all stories end happily, the opportunity for change exists.

The stories of the five mothers presented in this book are typical of those that I have heard over the past eighteen years. By giving readers an intimate, first-hand glimpse into the lives of these families, we hope to bring family homelessness beyond the shelter wall and into the public eye. We hope it will lead us one step further towards ending our nation's homeless family crisis.

Leonard N. Stern

June 2004
New York City

ACKNOWLEDGEMENTS

Today homelessness is so much more than just a housing issue. It is a multidimensional sketch of life and poverty. Personal lives that have moved in many directions and for one reason or another resulted in episodes of homelessness. This work offers a snapshot of that process; its' stories are real, in many cases puzzling and in a number of ways disheartening.

This book would not have been possible without the hard work of the staff of the Institute for Children and Poverty in New York City. Special thanks to my research assistant, Naomi Sugie, who performed numerous hours of personal interviews with homeless families. And to Laura Caruso, Karina Kwok, and Jesse Ellison goes credit for putting up with so many rewrites and editorial changes. Their insights were invaluable.

But above all, this project would have never happened if it were not for Leonard N. Stern, founder of Homes for the Homeless and the Institute for Children and Poverty, who never hesitates to ask the difficult questions, and who always pushes forward into uncharted waters. His inspiration and support has been the heart of Homes for the Homeless. Many thanks.

Ralph da Costa Nunez
New York City

INTRODUCTION

Beginning in the early 1980s, the federal government reduced its commitment to affordable housing programs as poor neighborhoods gentrified. Low-skilled and blue-collared jobs were outsourced as the national economy went global; cuts in federal aid programs removed the safety net for many low-income families; and for the first time, parents and children were fast becoming the norm rather than the exception among the homeless. In 1980, slightly less than 1,000 families lived in New York City shelters; today, there are more than 9,000. And the National Conference of Mayors reports that nationally nearly ninety percent (88%) of all major cities expect significant increases in emergency shelter requests over the next twelve months. This year alone, an estimated 3.5 million people in the United States will be homeless, with the fastest growing segment being young mothers and children.[1]

But as more and more families continue to seek shelter, family homelessness remains a confusing social issue. National statistics demonstrate that it is not simply an affordable housing problem but is symptomatic of a new American poverty—a chronic, intergenerational poverty fueled by failed educational systems and cutbacks in government social programs. In New York City today, more than half (55%) of homeless parents have not finished high school, and less than two percent (1.5%) completed any higher education.[2] Most grew up in unstable and oftentimes traumatizing environments. One in four (26%) suffered from family violence; one in three (33%) lived apart from their own parents as children, mostly in foster care; and nearly ten percent (9.4%) were themselves homeless growing up.[3]

For these parents, the cycle of instability is likely to pass to their own sons and daughters. One in ten homeless children have been left back in school, and more than half (55%) transferred schools within one year. Of these, twenty-one percent (21%) transferred twice and sixteen percent (16%) transferred three times or more, all as the direct results of being homeless.[4] As for their health, these children are nearly six times more likely to suffer from asthma (40% versus the national average of 7%) and three times more likely to develop gastrointestinal disorders (15% versus 4%).[5]

Unlike single adults living on the streets, homeless families are largely invisible to the public, doubling-up in already overcrowded housing or sleeping in shelters. The collection of personal stories that follows gives a face to this oftentimes hidden population. Five homeless mothers living in New York City shelters were interviewed over the course of a year. And while they were randomly selected, each story is compelling but no different from the experiences of other women living in the shelter system today. The intimate portraits detail stories of abuse, violence, housing instability, childhood trauma, immigration, poor education, young motherhood, addiction disorders, and an all-encompassing, entrenched poverty. In their own words, they describe the events that eventually led to their homelessness and help to clarify how family homelessness has become much more than just a housing problem.

NOTES

1 U.S. Conference of Mayors, *Sodexho Hunger and Homelessness Survey 2003*, December 2003; Martha R. Burt, "What Will It Take To End Homelessness?" *Urban Institute*, October 2001. <http://www.urban.org>.

2 Institute for Children and Poverty, 2003 Demographic Survey, unpublished.

3 2003 Demographic Survey.

4 Institute for Children and Poverty, *Homeless in America: A Children's Story*, 1999.

5 McLean, Diane E., et al. "Asthma Among Homeless Children." *Archives of Pediatrics and Adolescent Medicine*. March 2004: 158: 244. <http:// www.archpediatrics.com>; Institute for Children and Poverty, "Déjà vu: Family Homelessness in New York City," April 2001.

CHAPTER ONE
Rose, age 21

Teenage Pregnancy

Everybody says, "How do you cope with being in a shelter and knowing what you went through growing up and not knowing your real family?" It's hard but I take it a day at a time and I thank God that I'm here to see my own kids, and I wish that my mother was here to see her grandkids because she would be like, "Oh no! Where did all these kids come from?"

Rose is a slim, short, twenty-one year old with childlike features. She dresses casually, wears little to no makeup and holds her hair tightly away from her face with a bandana or in a ponytail. Rose has five children—a five-year-old son, a four-year-old daughter, two-year-old twin daughters, and a six-month-old boy. All, but the baby boy, are in foster care. Because she has spent most of her childhood with adopted families and in group homes, she is determined to prevent her own children from getting caught in the same foster care system. "I am fighting to make sure that I get my kids back. They are in the same agency that I was in and that's the part I don't want to happen...I'm not going to give them up."

Life with Heavenly

Even today, Rose is trying to piece together the events of her early childhood. Her brother and sister have provided certain details—her father's first name is Robert, her mother died from a drug overdose when Rose was four years old, and her grandmother suffered from a liver problem and could not raise the children. Aside from these details, Rose does not remember much. Although she often refers to her mother as deceased, she is not completely convinced her mother is dead. "In my heart, I still believe that she's somewhere out there and she just couldn't deal with the situation…She felt that someone else could take better care of us than she could."

Rose assumes that her grandmother, too ill to raise the children and unable to find other relatives, put her and her siblings up for adoption. Different families adopted each of the three children; at age four, Rose went to live with Heavenly, an older woman who was already raising a large family. Among all of the children and grandchildren that lived in Heavenly's house, she was the youngest and the only adopted child. She felt like an outsider and was treated differently compared to the other children. She believes that Heavenly adopted her because of financial benefits rather than more beneficent purposes, remembering her as "more like the devil" than a saintly person. To avoid Heavenly's frequent abuse, Rose often ran away from home, seeking refuge at the nearby elementary school. She remembers the police finding her, only to return her to Heavenly's violence. "I was so little. I was the littlest one in the house and she would hit me and I used to run away from her and they would put me back in the house."

When the beatings became too unbearable, Rose ran away to live at various group homes. She went to the ones that were anonymous and did not require names. "I liked it in the group homes. I made friends. I felt safe and nobody was picking on me." After staying at group homes for brief periods of time, Rose would return to Heavenly.

In junior high school, she became good friends with a girl named Joanne. "I used to hang out with her. Everyday after school I would go to her house and then leave and go home...I didn't know where else to go so I went to her house." Eventually, Rose was spending most of the day at Joanne's house in order to escape the violence at home.

Rose repeatedly asked Joanne if she could live with her family; however, Joanne did not seem to realize the severity of Rose's situation and did not take the requests seriously. When Rose came to school with a black eye, Joanne finally understood why she always wanted to go to her house after school and why she seemed hesitant to return home. Joanne took her to their junior high school counselor who finally intervened. "If it wasn't for my counselor helping me, I would never be with the family that I am with [now]." At age twelve, after eight years of living with Heavenly, Rose moved into Joanne's house and Joanne's mother became her legal guardian. Rose was now the youngest of five new siblings—two sisters and three brothers.

To this day, she considers Joanne's family as her own. Although they have their difficulties, Rose and her mother communicate well and have formed a close bond over the past nine years. "We have our ups and downs but we do keep a good relationship. We try to keep everything open and I care about her so much."

Still a Child

While in eighth grade Rose started dating Steve, a boy that she knew since elementary school and had previously dated. Steve did not return for school in the fall and it was only by coincidence that Rose ran into him on the street, more than a year later. "I was walking home from school and I heard somebody holler at me. I looked back and I was shocked. I was like, 'Where have you been?'"

For Steve, the past year had been a traumatic landslide of events: he was hit by a car, requiring months of rehabilitation on his legs, and his family entered the New York City shelter system. They were now living in a transitional family shelter two blocks away from Rose's apartment. She started spending her days and evenings at Steve's shelter. "My mother was like, 'You can't be going to see him all of the time. You got school, you got to do this, and you got to do that.' I was like, 'But that's my boyfriend and I love him.'" When Steve's family found an apartment in Queens, Rose ran away from her mother's place in Harlem to live with him. Her mother came out to Queens to bring her back home; however, Rose insisted on staying close to her boyfriend. She chose independence from her mother's demands by entering a group home in Staten Island rather than returning home.

By coincidence, Rose checked herself into the same group home that her biological sister Nelly had left earlier that day. "The same day that I went to that group home [was] the same day that my sister just got packed and was leaving." When a staff person at the group home informed Rose that she had just missed seeing Nelly, she was devastated; she had not seen her for over ten years.

Going to the group home was full of surprising discoveries. After her mandatory physical, it was the group home's medical examiner that told Rose that she was pregnant. At fifteen years old, she was frightened and confused. When she told her mother about the pregnancy, her mother was shocked. "She was like, wow. She couldn't believe it but she was like, it's your choice. I said that I wanted to keep him because it was a boy and she was happy because it was her first grandchild." Although relations with her mother were fine, Rose continued to live at the group home for the next few months. During this time, she told Steve and his family the news—she was going through with the pregnancy and Steve was the father. "He was happy but his mother disapproved because she felt that her son was too young to have a child." After becoming pregnant, Rose rarely saw Steve and to this day, she does not understand why he vanished from her life. "His family basically told him that it wasn't his so I guess he felt that way but I didn't really know. I didn't know how he was feeling because he didn't really come to me or talk to me." Last year, Rose heard that Steve was killed in a gang-related shooting.

Rose returned home in time for her junior high school graduation ceremony. Miraculously, she had managed to keep up with schoolwork and attend classes even though the Staten Island group home was hours away by ferry and subway to her Harlem-based school.

Struggling in School

In her eighth month of pregnancy, Rose entered high school. Starting over at a new school was difficult, especially since she was visibly pregnant, but she met a group of older students who helped her maintain healthy eating habits at school. "They noticed that I wasn't eating because I didn't know anybody and they used to sit there and make me eat: 'you're pregnant. You're going to eat.'" By the end of the first month of school, Rose had given birth to a healthy baby boy, Darrell. "When I finally had my son, they all came to the hospital to visit me. I was so happy. They were just making me laugh. I had a c-section so every time they would make me laugh, I would cry afterwards."

Soon after she returned from the hospital, her biological siblings Nelly and Michael visited. Incredibly, Nelly found Rose's contact information after returning to the Staten Island group home. "[Nelly] brought me flowers, balloons; I was so happy!" Despite the joy of reuniting, Nelly brought sad news—their grandmother had died a few years earlier. "When I found out, I started crying because I always talked about my grandmother. When my grandmother had us, I felt safe." Since that surreal day, Rose has lost contact with Nelly and Michael. Her mother changed their phone number and with such unstable housing histories, Nelly and Michael seem to have disappeared from Rose's radar. Rose heard that Nelly may be in Texas, engaged to a football player, but the information is hearsay.

With the support of her family, Rose was able to continue attending high school. "My father wasn't working at the time [so] he watched Darrell; he was the babysitter for me. When I came home—I came straight home from school—I did my homework and I just took care of him after that." She remembers her high school days as sleepless. Like most babies, Darrell cried every night, preventing Rose and Joanne from getting a full night's rest. "My sister and I were in the same room so she was like, 'I got to go to sleep! I got to go to school!'" Joanne and Rose would often skip school because Darrell had kept them up at night.

Rose's new boyfriend Frank was also very helpful with raising Darrell. "He was there for the whole time that my son was born; my son grew up with him."

The Second Pregnancy

Rose and Frank had been dating for about one year when she discovered she was pregnant; she was sixteen years old. "I just knew because I started getting sick and getting tired. I went to the doctor." When Rose told Frank the news, he was happy and there was no question that she would go through with the pregnancy. As with Steve's mother, Frank's mother was upset. "His mother was telling him, 'that's not yours.' She didn't really like me like that." Unlike Steve, Frank remained actively involved in the pregnancy. By this time, Rose had dropped out of high school and Frank, having already graduated, was working. When she went to the hospital to give birth, her mother held her hand and Frank waited right outside the room. "He didn't come into the room during the birth because he was scared…he was outside in the hallway praying." Rose's second child was a baby girl, Neesha. When Frank's mother saw Neesha for the first time, she could no longer deny that she had become a grandmother. "His mother was so happy. She was like, 'I got a granddaughter!'"

As parents, Rose and Frank tried to create a more traditional family life. They lived together; however, financial constraints forced them to live with Rose's family in their already-crowded apartment. In the beginning, life with Frank was okay. "We got along and everything. He was going and doing what he had to do—going to work." But after two years of being together, Rose realized that he had been cheating on her and keeping secrets from her. "He wasn't trying to help me. He was basically worried about his friends and cheating on people. He wanted to play games and…I think he was always [cheating], it was just that I didn't know before." When Rose found out about the infidelities and confronted Frank, he became violent. Looking back on the confrontation, she says, "I could never let a man hit me. I fought back. Even though people always say, you should not fight back, I wasn't going to hear that. I nearly killed him."

Refocused

After her relationship with Frank ended, Rose decided that she needed to get her life back on track. "I said, screw you. I'm going to go get a job and fix myself up." After watching a television advertisement for Covenant House, she decided to go to the transitional shelter for homeless and at-risk youth, hoping to benefit from their wide range of support services. Her mother agreed to take care of Darrell and Neesha while she enrolled in job training programs through Covenant House. "They helped me a lot because I did have three jobs at times when I wanted. They also help you while you're working. They help you save your money so when you find an apartment you could have money on the side."

While living at Covenant House, Rose met a new boy, Victor. "He was nice because he really didn't talk to nobody. He stayed to himself and he would always listen to music. With him, he doesn't go up to girls to talk to them. He lets them come to him." Victor's laid-back behavior was a refreshing change from Frank's more aggressive, sure-shot attitude. When Frank heard that Rose was dating someone new, he was extremely jealous and even went as far as asking Rose to marry him. "I said no because I knew how he was and I wasn't going to go into something that he wasn't ready for. I said, 'you're just doing that because you know that I'm with somebody else and you don't want to see me with nobody else.'"

After six months of living in Covenant House, Rose returned to her mother's home. Although Covenant House was a positive experience overall, she felt that "a lot of kids started to come in because they thought it was a hang-out place to get away from their families, and after a while it was getting too out of hand." Around the same time, Victor also left Covenant House to live at a different shelter. Soon after she returned home, Rose discovered that she was pregnant with twins. With the negative reactions of the fathers' families from her previous pregnancies, she worried about what Victor and his family would say about this pregnancy, her third pregnancy in four years. Rose decided to not tell Victor about the twins until after giving birth. "He didn't know at the time that I was pregnant with the twins. I never told him because I was scared about how he might react."

Turning to the EAU

With three-year-old Darrell, two-year-old Neesha, two more babies on the way, no steady boyfriend to rely on, and no job to provide income, Rose felt trapped. She knew that after the twins were born, her mother's overcrowded apartment would be too small for the extra additions. Rose thought that she needed her own apartment but with no current job and no prospects of retaining a job in the fore-seeable future, finding an apartment would be impossible. Rose's mother, who had gone through the New York City shelter system years earlier and had found her current apartment through the process, urged her to apply for shelter at the Emergency Assistance Unit (EAU). "My mother told me about [the EAU] and said, 'well, that's the only way that you're going to get your place. You keep try-ing to work but you got too many kids and you're going to have bills and bills so you might as well go through the EAU and get it done like that. At least you have a place to stay.' She basically took me through [the shelter system process] because I didn't want to go through the EAU. I was like, is there any other way besides going there?"

With her mother watching Darrell and Neesha, Rose went to the EAU. She still vividly remembers that first experience. "It was gross in the EAU. It was filthy in there. Kids got asthma, seizures, everybody was sick in there." After days of sitting in the waiting room and nights of moving back and forth between overnight hotels, Rose, weak after refusing to eat the nauseating EAU food, was placed in a transitional family shelter. Because she had never previously received public assistance, she needed to first apply for welfare before contin-uing through the shelter system process. Rose spent most of her days on the subways, traveling to her welfare office and obtaining the nec-essary documents in order to start receiving public assistance. Stressed from trying to apply, she became ill. "I was really sick. I had pneu-monia and a throat infection."

Rose's doctor told her that she was too sick to continue in the shelter system, the health of her twins were in jeopardy, and if she had alternative housing options, she should use them. Before Rose's application for welfare was approved, she left the shelter system and returned to her mother's house. When Rose finally gave birth to healthy twin daughters, she allowed only her mother into the birthing room. Because of her pregnancy, she could not take the appropriate medicine to fight her pneumonia. "I was really sick and didn't want anybody around me." Only after her health returned did Rose contact Victor and tell him about his twin daughters. She was convinced that Victor was the father; however, Frank insisted the babies were his. "I knew who the father was because I was with [Victor] and I wasn't with Frank. Frank just didn't want to hear that I got pregnant by somebody else."

ACS Intervenes

It was generally understood that Rose's newborn twins were Victor's daughters, causing Frank to become even more jealous and upset. One evening, he unexpectedly arrived at Rose's mother's apartment, and a noisy and fierce argument ensued. Rose believes that a neighbor, hearing the argument between her and Frank, called ACS to report suspected violence in the household. A couple of days later, Administration for Children's Services (ACS) arrived to interrogate Rose about the home environment.

ACS workers did not find abuse in the apartment but they did find overcrowded conditions and threatened to charge Rose with parental neglect because of inadequate housing. "They felt that my mother's house was too small so all of us couldn't be there. They said that I could go [back] to Covenant House with my twins while my mother kept the oldest two." Nineteen-year-old Rose knew that she needed employment to find proper housing for herself and her four children so she again turned to Covenant House for help. After a couple of months of living at Covenant House, working at a minimum wage job, and leaving her twins with the daycare center at Covenant House, she decided to leave due to personal problems with the daycare staff and to move into Victor's family's house in Staten Island.

ACS did not agree with this new housing arrangement and felt that Rose was inadequately caring for her four children. Rose herself admits that she was not involved in her children's lives at this time. It was agreed that her mother would have temporary custody of all four children and she would move back into the house to help raise the children. Sharing parental control created power struggles and arguments for Rose and her mother. "I helped out with the kids but at the time, [my mother] wasn't letting me do anything. She was trying to be 'mommy' instead of letting me be 'mommy.' I didn't like that so I told the ACS worker." Upon re-evaluation of the situation, ACS decided that neither Rose nor her mother was properly caring for the children. Rose was not actively involved in her children's lives and her mother had a developing drug and substance abuse problem, grounds for removing the children from the home. When Rose's mother learned that ACS intervened at Rose's request, she blamed her for the children's removal. "My mother was upset. She was mad at me. She felt that, for some part, it was my fault, [but] if she would have given me a chance to raise my kids, I wouldn't have told."

Foster Care

Although ACS tried to keep Rose's four children together, Darrell and Neesha ended up living with one foster family while the twins went to another family. In the beginning, Rose, frustrated and bitter that ACS "betrayed" her by removing her children, refused to attend the mandated parenting classes. "I thought it wasn't my fault so why did I have to do everything? Those are *my* kids." However, returning the children was conditional on her completion of these programs and after a few months, Rose realized that she needed to follow ACS's instructions if she wanted to regain custody of her four children. "They told me that if I didn't do [the parenting classes], I wasn't going to get my kids back so I said, well, I might as well do it and get it over with to show them that I am doing something and that I do want my kids back." Around the same time, she discovered that she was pregnant with a baby boy; Victor was the father. Once again, she realized that her life needed reevaluation. She and Victor attended parenting skills programs, but Rose still did not have appropriate housing for her children to be returned. "Me and [Victor] did parenting classes and after that, ACS said that I still had to have housing. So we said that we might as well go to the EAU together."

Rose's decision to go to the EAU a second time was not quite as easy as she makes it sound. Before returning to the shelter system she and Victor looked for apartments in the paper, but with Victor's small income from Supplemental Security Income (SSI) for his chronic seizures, they quickly realized that every suitable apartment was out of their meager price range. She and Victor turned to the EAU because they believed that they "had no place else to live." According to Rose, "[going through the shelter system] was the only way that I could get my kids back. [ACS] told me that I had to go through the EAU."

Returning to the EAU

When twenty-year-old Rose entered the EAU for a second time, her four children were in foster care and she was pregnant with her fifth child. "It was really hard. Everything was stressful—no money and going to the appointments that they wanted us to go to. It was hard, really hard. I was trying to figure out what it was going to be, either go through it together or leave and try to work something out." Rose and Victor decided to continue through the shelter system. She remembers sitting in the EAU, crying because of the stress and hungry because the provided food was oftentimes spoiled. "The pregnant women—we'd all be there crying because it was so stressful being pregnant and not having enough money to eat. I mean, eating the food was so nasty! A lot of kids got sick, a lot of kids got put in the hospital."

The provided meals and high stress level were reminiscent of her first time at the EAU; however this time was different—Rose was not alone. She and Victor applied together as a family, with Victor financially supporting Rose. In addition to Victor's companionship, Rose ran into a number of friends that were also applying for emergency shelter. She likened the experience to a high school reunion. "When I was in the EAU, I saw a lot of familiar faces that I knew—friends from school, from high school—and they were like, 'You're going through this too?'" Rose estimates that about ten friends have applied for shelter at the EAU.

In fact, entering the emergency shelter system is not uncommon among Rose's family. In addition to her mother's application years ago, her sister Joanne had gone to the EAU a few months prior to Rose's entry. Joanne had given birth to her first child and needed more space than the cramped quarters of her boyfriend's family's house. "[Joanne] thought that she could go back to my mother's house but my mother was like, well, you have to go to the EAU so [ACS] won't say anything." Rose's mother was trying to regain temporary custody of the children and believed that ACS would grant her custody conditional on adequate housing. However, when ACS visited the house, they decided not to grant custody to her mother "[When ACS] changed their minds about letting my mother get [the children] back, my mother told [Joanne] that she could come back home." For Joanne, the "germs" floating around the EAU, the institutional living, and the stress of constantly waiting to be approved for housing were too overwhelming, and she returned home as soon as her mother allowed her.

Life in the Shelter System

Rose and Victor were determined to make it through the shelter system and obtain a housing subsidy because they viewed these goals as synonymous with regaining custody of the children. While moving back and forth between the EAU and temporary overnight placements was difficult, Rose's mother's support eased the process. "If we needed our clothes washed, we'd come to [my mother's] house, wash our clothes, take showers, and go back to the EAU." Whenever she or Victor was able to get a pass to leave the EAU for a few hours, they would go to her mother's house. After shuttling between the EAU, her mother's house, and their overnight hotel placements for ten days, Rose and Victor's application for emergency shelter was denied. EAU investigators believed that she could return to her mother's house. "They felt like we had somewhere to stay…if they think that there's a corner of the house then they'll tell you that you can stay there."

Rose and Victor's application was rejected once more before being approved. "I had to literally get a notarized letter from the court stating that I couldn't go back to my mother." Rose and Victor moved to a maternity home and a couple months after living in the shelter system, she gave birth to a healthy boy, Marcus. Because she was still not receiving public assistance, Victor supported the family on his SSI payments. "He had all the money. I didn't really have anything…he bought the crib, clothes—everything." Because of Victor's position, Rose agreed to file all of their EAU paperwork under his name.

Soon after Rose gave birth, Victor, already stressed from fatherhood, shelter life, and outside family issues, had an accident. "He fell down a flight of stairs in a train station and in the process of that, he went into a seizure. And the same day that he fell, his uncle died so when his mother called him and told him that, he just bugged out." Victor checked himself into the psychiatric ward of the nearby hospital and when he returned to the shelter, he refused to continue taking his medication to control his seizures. The effects of not taking his medication were immediate. "He was having seizures and he started talking to himself…he was like a baby—he didn't do things, he didn't go nowhere and I couldn't deal with that. He wanted me to run back and forth with him to the hospital and I couldn't do it. I had just had my baby so how could I help him?…He hit me and that's when I said, I can't deal with this. You got to go."

Shelter staff forced him to leave and the police arrested him. A few days later, Victor returned to the shelter, threatening to kill her. Flustered and upset, Rose and her baby transferred to a new shelter in the Bronx. Today, she attributes Victor's sudden change in behavior to his refusal to take his medication and does not blame him for the violent outbursts. "He just didn't know who he was. He was really out of it."

On Their Own

Rose and Marcus have lived at their current Bronx shelter for the past seven months; Rose herself has been in the shelter system for over eighteen months, more than three times DHS's projected goal of a six-month shelter stay. Because Rose initially applied for housing with Victor and did not know that he had a criminal record, her application was denied. She appealed the court's decision, filed a new housing application, and was recently approved for a rent subsidy.

Rose and Marcus are familiar faces around the Bronx shelter and are very friendly with other residents and staff. Marcus resembles his mother, being quick to laugh and having Rose's easy-going smile. Last month, Marcus celebrated his one-year birthday; he has spent his entire young life growing up in the shelter system. People often comment that mother and child are attached at the hip—Rose is never without Marcus and always watches him during the day rather than putting him in the shelter's daycare program or having a fellow resident baby-sit. Watching Rose take care of Marcus, it is hard to imagine her as a neglectful or uncaring parent; however, it is also hard to imagine how such a young person—Rose is now twenty one years old—could raise five children.

These days, Rose is very busy looking for a suitable apartment to rent, taking ACS-mandated parenting classes and domestic violence classes, and going to counseling. She keeps in contact by telephone with the foster families of Darrell, Neesha, and the twins, and sees her children during brief bi-weekly visits. According to ACS, once Rose obtains an apartment, she will get weekend visits with her children until she proves competent as a parent. Only then will she receive a subsidy for a larger apartment and will have to look for a new apartment to accommodate herself and five children.

While Rose spends most of her time working to regain custody of her children, she has also been going to court in order to prevent Frank from gaining custody of four-year-old Neesha. Ever since Neesha entered the foster care system two years ago, Frank and his mother have taken Rose to court numerous times. "Once his child got into the system, he blamed it all on me." Despite Frank's efforts in court, Rose believes that his lack of effort outside of court sends a louder message to ACS. Like Rose, he has requirements to fulfill such as parenting classes, a psychiatric evaluation, and follow-up meetings with ACS in order to prove his ability as a responsible adult and qualified parent. Not only has he failed to complete these requirements, he has also stopped attending the biweekly visits with his daughter. "Now that he has stopped visiting her, how is she supposed to feel?...He's not taking the effort to come and see her and I'm not going to sit there and force her on to him. She doesn't like her father. She has said, "Mommy, I don't like Daddy." And I was like, Why? 'He don't come to see me no more,' that's what she said." Rose does not understand why Frank continues to pursue the case in court if he is unwilling to repair his personal relationship with Neesha.

Hopes for the Future

Despite the hardships and difficulties Rose has faced through-out her young life, she is optimistic for the future. "I think about what happened growing up but I try to not think about it too much because in some ways, I feel better now that I'm safe and I'm old enough to make my own decisions." Like many women in the shelter system, Rose believes that her ability to continue in the system is a sign of strength and she views the process as another hurdle she must cross in order to regain custody of her children. "Sometimes I would just really feel like giving up and going back home and I didn't do that because I have four children [in foster care]. I came through [the shelter system] because I wanted to get my own place and get my children to live with me." Even with five children and no high school diploma, Rose hopes that she will establish a successful career as a lawyer. She is trying to get her GED, but after testing below the junior high school proficiency level, she will have to take a pre-GED class before enrolling in the regular program. "I want to be a lawyer. I say to people, 'never say never.' I'm only twenty-one; I've got a whole lifetime to go."

Soon after celebrating her 22nd birthday, Rose discovered she was pregnant with her sixth child. As a result, her ACS case is now stalled and she does not know if she will receive custody of her other children in the near future. According to her caseworker, she is devastated.

....

In the last year alone, teenage pregnancy rates in New York City shelters increased from thirty-seven percent (37%) to forty-seven percent (47%)—nearly five times higher than the citywide average and nearly ten times higher than the national rate.[1] Of these young mothers, forty-one percent (41%) lived apart from their parents, thirty-nine percent (39%) witnessed domestic violence, and twenty-five percent (25%) were physically abused while growing up. Fifty-three percent (53%) were themselves the children of adolescent parents.[2]

Children of teenage mothers are fifty percent (50%) more likely to repeat a grade and less likely to score well on standardized tests or complete high school.[3] Further, homeless children are sixty percent (60%) more likely to be removed from parental care (16% versus 10%), a reflection of young mothers' ill-equipped parenting skills. Children raising children can only continue the cycle of young motherhood, instability, and poverty.

NOTES

1 In 2000, New York City's teen pregnancy rate was 9.9%, while the rate for the United States was 5%.

2 Institute For Children and Poverty, "Children Having Children: Teen Pregnancy and Homelessness in New York City," April 2003.

3 National Campaign to Prevent Teen Pregnancy, "Teen Pregnancy —So What?" February 2004: 3. <http://www.teenpregnancy.org>.

CHAPTER TWO
Anita, age 24

Foster Care

They took the youngest ones first and when that day came for me to go, I was excited as hell. I ran outside. I jumped in the van. My grandmother came running after: "Wait! You need some clothes!"

"I don't need nothing lady! We don't need nothing! They say they've got everything; they've got food!" I was so excited...

Anita left her grandmother's house on December 31, 1990. She was eleven years old when the foster care van came to take her and her eight brothers and sisters to new foster homes. For Anita, foster care offered an escape from the daily abuse that she experienced living with her grandmother, aunt, and uncle. She eagerly welcomed the foster care system; however, her oldest brother Jamal knew better. At the time, Jamal was fourteen years old, and he had heard what foster care was like; he decided to run.

A Mother Too Young

While still in her teens, Anita's mother gave birth to the first of her nine children and began her long and rocky relationship with drugs until her death in 2002; she was forty-two years old. Despite her "horrible, horrible childhood," Anita is not resentful of her mother's neglect. "I'm not going to say that she didn't really care because it was something that she couldn't control." After each child was born, Anita's mother would pass the baby to her own mother's house. Eventually, all nine children lived with their grandmother in Brooklyn. There, they were subject to their alcoholic grandmother's physical abuse and their cocaine-addicted aunt and uncle's sexual abuse.

"My grandmother always made my nose bleed. She was hitting us all of the time." Anita was very fearful of her grandmother. Even as an older child, she often wet her bed at night. In the morning, her grandmother would beat her and in turn, the accidents would become more and more frequent. Today, Anita still vividly remembers her grandmother's violence and recounts one incident in particular, in which she desperately wanted a new book bag. It was leather with the word "Brooklyn" embroidered on the front. It was hip and trendy, and when her grandmother finally agreed to buy her the bag, Anita was thrilled. Within the week, however, it was torn. "I threw it over the chair in the music room and there was a big rip on the side of the bag. I was scared to death." She took the bag to her aunt.

"Can you sew it up for me? Please don't tell."

Although her aunt promised to keep the secret, she soon betrayed Anita's trust. Furious, her grandmother gave Anita a severe beating, which she would never forget.

After experiencing eleven years of neglect, violence, and sexual abuse, Human Resources Administration's Bureau of Child Welfare (BCW)[1] finally intervened. Anita's younger sister Darlene was the only child who had constant contact with her father's side; her family had noticed the permanent array of welts, bruises, and marks scattered over Darlene's small frame. After discovering signs of physical and sexual abuse on the children, the BCW removed them from their grandmother's home. As the children piled into the foster care van, Anita's grandmother ran after them:

"I never beat the kids! Nobody touched them! It was the families on their fathers' side!"

Anita remembers herself thinking, "What was my grandmother going to say about me? I didn't see [my father's] family so what was she going to say?"

In Foster Care

"We all have different fathers—all nine of us. Some of our fathers were in our lives and some just weren't; some couldn't be found.[2] My brother Erwin, his father wanted him and he went to South Carolina. My sister Darlene, her father took her and they went to North Carolina. My other sisters and brothers, they were all adopted by the foster families that they were living with. They were all little. I'm the only one that didn't get adopted. I had serious psychiatric problems that no one wanted to deal with."

Initially, Anita and her sisters were placed together with a foster family in the Bronx. In the beginning, she liked her foster placement; however, it was difficult to start her life over with a new family in a strange home. "They weren't mean; they were very, very nice. *I was mean, very rebellious* ... I started lashing out. I don't remember why—maybe the fact of us being there or being treated differently—I didn't know that it was going to be like that. I started throwing dressers and terrorizing people. I was really terrorizing the people!"

After a few months, Anita was separated from her sisters and transferred to a group home in Brentwood, Long Island. The new home did little to ease her anger and violent tendencies; she was soon placed in a psychiatric hospital in Long Island. By this time, Anita was thirteen years old. "It was horrible. Months and months of medication, hospitalization, needles, straightjackets, locked up in the room, no one comes to visit me for eight, nine, ten months at a time. My birthday passed and I never got anything." Anita remembers herself as the "ugliest, the skinniest, and the tallest," and believed that nobody liked her because she was new. She recalls the taunting: "Anita's a boy. She's always wearing high waters. She's too skinny. She's so skinny that she could hula-hoop through a cheerio!" Anita rarely went outside and days were slow moving. "Take your medication, watch TV, do arts and crafts, go to therapy, take medication, take a nap, eat…"

Because of her violent and erratic behavior, she would be moved from psychiatric hospital to foster family to group home and back to psychiatric hospital every few months. For the next nine years, Anita would live in fourteen different foster homes, five psychiatric hospitals, two group homes, and three residential centers. For the most part, her memory of her childhood and adolescence is foggy. "I remember a lot of the homes of where I was at. I just don't remember where it was, what were the names of the people, and what year it was. All I can remember are the faces, like jerry-curl-lady who's always drinking ice tea with fifteen packs of sugar and smoking cigarettes." Anita's stays with the various foster families were never more than a few months and she spent most of her adolescence within the confines of large institutions.

Becoming A Mother

While living in one of the residential centers, sixteen-year-old Anita discovered that she was pregnant. She was transferred to a maternity home and after feeling pressure from BCW to either have an abortion or give up the baby, decided not to go through with the pregnancy. "They were trying to scare me and it succeeded." Soon after leaving the maternity home, she was placed in yet another foster home.

Her new foster mother was a young twenty-three-year-old woman who was already raising other foster children in addition to kids of her own. Anita was a mature-looking seventeen year old and the oldest child in the family; her foster mother's boyfriend would constantly try to "hook her up" with his friends, and Anita would repeatedly reject his offers at matchmaking. Soon after moving into this new home, Anita's foster mother's boyfriend, high on drugs, raped her. When she told her foster mother what had happened, her foster mother tried to protect her boyfriend and ignore Anita's claims. She sent Anita to her mother's house and Anita continued to live with her foster "grandmother" for the next few weeks.

It is around this time that Anita dropped out of high school; she was in the twelfth grade. Incredibly, she had kept up with her schoolwork until now. Each time BCW sent her to another foster home or group home, Anita started over at a new school. At this point, trying to catch up on schoolwork became too overwhelming. "I just left high school because of all the things I was going through—it was like out of a movie or something and it was really difficult to keep trying to focus in school."

Depressed and unsure of what her next step should be, Anita began drinking heavily and incessantly smoking marijuana. At the time, she did not know that she was pregnant with her foster mother's boyfriend's child. "I remember that I went out to smoke some weed and I felt tired so I went back into the building. As I was walking, I started feeling really hot—really, really hot. I took off my winter coat and I was just burning up. I got into the building, got into the elevator, made it upstairs to the floor, and as soon as they opened the door, I just passed out. I didn't know that I was pregnant." Anita was taken to the hospital and when she told hospital staff that her pregnancy was the result of a rape, BCW immediately launched an investigation.

Even now, Anita is unsure of the police investigation's outcome. She knows that BCW temporarily took away her foster mother's children—both her biological children and her foster children— but she believes that her perpetrator was never formally charged with the rape. At the time of the investigation, Anita's energy was consumed by her own battle against BCW, who was pressuring her to abort her pregnancy or give her child up for adoption. "They were saying that if I had the baby, they weren't going to let me keep her." When BCW workers interrogated her about her reasons for keeping her baby, they told her that her answers were "dumb" and "didn't make sense." Anita felt as though she was on trial for becoming pregnant and thus, for being raped.

BCW workers tried to convince Anita that she would fail as a mother, that she would end up losing her child to the foster care system, and that she was just too young. However, she refused to get an abortion. She was still struggling with the very recent experience of her first abortion, and as a product of the foster system, she refused to give her baby up for adoption. As a strange "bonus" to keeping her baby, Anita believed that having a child would protect and improve the conditions of her own life. "It was like I was using the pregnancy as a *pawn* for them to stop bothering me: you can't give me all of this medicine because I'm pregnant; you can't send me to this place because of the condition I'm in; you have to do this for me because of what I'm going through; don't tell me that I cannot have any clothes or money—I can't fit anything. I used it. I took advantage of it. I thought about it."

Throughout the term of her pregnancy, from her third month until delivery, Anita stayed at a maternity home in Manhattan. After leaving the hospital, she and her eight-pound, four-ounce daughter Claire were sent to a new foster family in upstate New York.

Today, six-year-old Claire still has not yet asked about her father, but Anita worries about the day she becomes curious. "If she asks, I don't even know what to say. 'I met him while I was in foster care. He was my foster mother's boyfriend. Let me tell you what happened, one day…' I can't tell her shit like that. I can't tell her that. That's horrible for a girl to find out. It would give a child nightmares; I had nightmares for a very long time, for years."

Foster Homes

Anita believes that BCW sent her and Claire to upstate New York in order for the city agency to avoid public scandal regarding the rape. But looking back on the experience with this new placement, she feels that this family, out of all her foster families, was the only one she liked. The foster mother seemed very excited that Anita and Claire had joined their family, and she even bought Anita a new sweater as an early birthday present. The sweater, however, quickly disappeared and soon after, her brief sense of stability deteriorated into depression over her recent past and anxiety about motherhood. Anita quickly realized that not only did she need to take care of Claire but also she needed to look after her own health. "Everything changed—my way of doing things. No more smoking and drinking like I used to, more responsibility now. The whole world just seemed different. I wasn't free anymore...I had responsibilities."

Stressed and exhausted from attending to Claire, Anita began constantly fighting with her other foster siblings. When the missing sweater mysteriously reappeared in her closet a month later, she accused her younger foster sister. "It was really stained and it smelled just like the girl's odor. I got mad. I tried to choke her with the funky sweater—with the funky sweater that she stole and that smelled like her. I was going to choke her with her own funk, that's what I kept telling her."

Anita packed her belongings, took Claire in her arm, and left her foster family. She called the police from a nearby neighbor's house, asking for help. Anita was subsequently institutionalized in a psychiatric hospital for two weeks; baby Claire stayed with the foster family during this time.

Anita and Claire were then placed with a different foster family upstate. Soon after moving into her new placement, Anita began to notice irregular behavior in her daughter. She told her foster mother but knowing Anita's past experiences with foster families, the foster mother was suspicious of her claims and hesitant to take Claire to the hospital. "The foster mother wouldn't tell me where the hospital was and she wouldn't even call the hospital for me." With her foster mother and father gone during one afternoon, Anita stole money from the house and took Claire, bleeding from her ears and nose, to the hospital's emergency room. "Had I known that the hospital was four blocks down the street, I wouldn't have stolen the damn money." Later that afternoon, with her daughter still in the hospital due to a hormone disorder, Anita returned to her foster home and was immediately arrested for theft.

She spent two months in a juvenile detention center while Claire stayed with the foster family. "The juvenile part was in the same place that the adults were in, it was just that, all the juveniles were in this big cage. It was in the corner of the jail and it was a metal, see-through cage like the fences on the street. There were two bunk beds, a shower, and a bathroom, and [the adults] could see everything, [such as] when we took our clothes off to get into the shower." While the center was a difficult and scary experience for Anita, she preferred it to some of her past placements in foster homes and psychiatric institutions. "I thought the jail was better than being in the homes and the hospitals. In jail, you didn't get in trouble for not taking medicine. You didn't need to take shit."

After serving two months, Anita was released to a group home in Brooklyn. Claire would stay in her foster home upstate and Anita would not regain custody of her daughter for another two years.

Starting Over

While Anita was in jail and in the Brooklyn group home, she started a relationship with Chris, a man in his early twenties that she met while in the psychiatric hospital upstate.

"The second day of me being in the hospital, they brought Chris. He walked from his Job Corps center[3] and the police picked him up ... He was walking so much that he walked the soles off of his boots." Dissatisfied with Job Corps, Chris had left the program and was wandering aimlessly through the dark roads upstate when the police picked him up and took him to the psychiatric ward of a nearby hospital.

After Chris was discharged, he returned to his mother's house in Queens. When he discovered that Anita had been placed in a group home in Brooklyn, he visited her often. "He was a nice friend and he hung out with me. I didn't want to live in a group home anymore. I wanted my daughter back. His mother said that I could stay with them and I went back to the group home to get my stuff."

Chris's home provided Anita with her own space and a rare feeling of ownership, unlike the group homes and hospitals; however, the old house was quickly deteriorating and by most judgments, physically uninhabitable. "It looked really nice on the outside but it was horrible on the inside. You were scared to walk up and down the stairs, there were big holes in the walls and bugs were crawling out the holes. There was a beehive in a hole in the wall of the basement and bees would be flying—big, giant ones. The sink had bad plumbing, the bathroom was horrible, and the shower wall was exposed. There was no heat. The kids were sleeping in one of the rooms but it was full of bugs and the kids kept getting bit up." Although Anita wanted to leave, she and Chris needed to save enough money to find their own place.

Soon after moving in with Chris, Anita discovered she was pregnant with his child. At twenty years old and expecting her second daughter, she began the long process of regaining custody of Claire. "What they put me through to get her back, it really changed my life." Anita went to parenting classes and frequent therapy sessions. "I had to prove to them that there was nothing wrong with me psychiatrically because I did come out of a hospital [and] the jail ... if there was any medication recommended for me to take, I had to take it. [Administration for Children's Services (ACS)] didn't want just a week or two of reports on my condition, they wanted six, seven, eight months of reports. It changed my life. It really changed my life."

Frustrated with her overworked Legal Aid attorney, Anita found a private lawyer to help get Claire back. Chris's mother paid for this new counsel and soon after hiring him, she regained full custody of Claire. Around the same time, Anita gave birth to her second daughter Thalia, and she and Chris began looking for an apartment of their own. As expected, ACS had declared Chris's mother's deteriorated house physically uninhabitable and Anita needed adequate housing for her two daughters.

A New Home, A New Family

After a long and difficult apartment search in Queens, Anita and Chris began looking for affordable apartments in other boroughs. They eventually moved to Brooklyn. It was the first apartment she had ever leased and it was the first time he had ever lived on his own and apart from his mother. Chris was working as a bus driver and Anita found a temporary job as a telemarketer. Claire was going to school and a close neighbor, Beth, watched Thalia and Claire when needed. For Anita, "It was the perfect life."

The fairy tale did not last long. After almost two years of living in Brooklyn, Chris' mother fell sick and he became depressed. Soon after, his driver's license was revoked for speeding; consequently, Chris lost his job as a bus driver. He became physically abusive and paranoid, thinking that Anita was lying about her commitment to their relationship. If the caller ID on their ringing telephone said "unavailable," Chris would refuse to let Anita answer the phone. Those callers were her "other boyfriends." If neighbors shouted "hey" or "yo" to them while walking down their street, he would blame Anita for being provocative. The worse was when Chris kept her awake in the middle of the night with his yelling. "At two o'clock in the morning, he would be sitting at the window, shouting, 'Nobody's going to touch my woman!'"

Thinking that Chris would recover from his paranoia if they moved back to his mother's house in Queens, Anita left the only apartment ever leased in her name. "I should have stayed in Brooklyn and let him move. We should have gone our separate ways from there. But instead, I gave up the apartment. I gave up the apartment to go back to Queens and I should have left him. It just got worse. He started picking up things to hit my kids and me." Soon after moving to Queens, Anita had found a job as a security guard at a nearby museum, but her chaotic home life caused her to be late or worse, to miss days from work, and she lost her job.

At one point, Chris's paranoia became too overwhelming for even himself to handle. In the middle of the night, Anita woke up and found him leaving the house; he had called 911. "He was walking out of the door. The ambulance was outside and he was getting in the truck. I said, 'Boy! Where are you going?'" Chris checked himself into the hospital's psychiatric ward and stayed there for a few weeks. With Chris gone, his mother asked Anita, Claire, and Thalia to leave. Anita turned to the Emergency Assistance Unit (EAU); however, she did not stay long enough to apply for shelter. "I only went in there for like, two minutes. I thought, I've seen enough. I've got to get out of here. I walked in and I walked out. It was stinking in there. I was like, this is not really for me." Anita called Chris at the hospital and he made arrangements for her to stay with his sister until he recovered. After a few weeks, Chris returned to his mother's place and Anita, Claire, and Thalia moved back into the dilapidated house.

When Chris began directing his violent outbursts toward her daughters, Anita decided that she had to leave. "He swung my daughter against the wall and my eyes—I think that they got the biggest they could ever go. I took the yellow pages book, it was heavy as hell, and I just kept hitting him with it until he picked up the ironing board and knocked me out … I called the police and had him arrested. I couldn't deal with it any longer."

After living with Chris for almost three years, Anita and her two daughters entered a shelter for domestic violence victims. While Claire is old enough to understand that Chris is dangerous, Thalia has mixed feelings toward her father. Now that Chris is scarcely a part of their lives, Thalia frequently talks about him: "Remember when Daddy picked up the ironing board, Mommy? And he hit you and you were crying? That's when the police came and they took my Daddy away ... and he was the *greatest guy*."

To this day, Anita wavers between thinking of Chris as a "bad person" and as a "decent person with a [mental] illness." Anita speculates about the causes for her deteriorated relationship. "I think it was because I had a past history of being with other guys and being in foster care and being beaten and smoking weed that really didn't appeal to him ... it was the illness that made us break up. It was this illness that made him put his hands on me."

Moving Back

"It was very hard to cope living in the domestic violence shelter because I wanted to leave—I wanted to leave him—but I didn't want to leave. I was still missing him a lot. I still loved him. My kids were always saying, 'When are we going back home?' It was really, really overwhelming and I was just crying all of the time and getting frustrated."

On the advice of the shelter's caseworkers, Anita signed Claire and Thalia into a respite home, which is a twenty-one day foster placement, and checked herself into a nearby hospital for mental health evaluations. "The doctors gave me some medicine to keep me calm. They said that my anxiety level was really high, that I was really depressed, and that I just needed some time for myself. The medicine had me so zonked out. I was so high that I couldn't do anything. I would just stand there and talk to you until my mouth started foaming. They had me talking a lot because of the medicine."

After a few days in the hospital, Anita returned to the shelter but kept Claire and Thalia in the respite home. Meanwhile, her grandmother contacted her with difficult news: her mother was very ill. More than twenty years of heavy drug and alcohol use had finally taken its toll on her mother's health. On the day she was supposed to pick up Claire and Thalia from the respite home, Anita visited her grandmother's house and attended to her mother. She arrived at the respite home after midnight and at the shelter after curfew. Because her daughters were not picked up on time, caseworkers filed a charge of child neglect with the Administration for Children's Services (ACS). The shelter discharged Anita for breaking curfew.

Alone, she moved back into her grandmother's house, the house she was so anxious to leave twelve years earlier. Her grandmother was still an alcoholic; her aunt and uncle were still drug addicted, "striving to get the next hit." Anita turned to marijuana. "Smoke weed, drink liquor ... that's all I ever did—smoke and drink, smoke and drink, smoke and drink. I was a straight-up pothead." Because of the child neglect charge, ACS had been monitoring Anita's mental stability and parenting skills. Adding drug use and mental instability to the charge of neglect, ACS removed Claire and Thalia from the house. Remembering her own experience with foster care, Anita fell into a deep depression after realizing what her kids were now experiencing.

After living at home a little over one month, Anita began to suspect she was pregnant. This would be her third child. While the father's identity is still unclear, she suspects her friend's cousin, a man

41

she was briefly involved with. Hearing that Anita may be pregnant, her friend urged her to go to the EAU as a means to get more appropriate housing. Anita's neighbor had been through it herself, a couple of years earlier, and received a Section 8 rent subsidy after months of living in emergency shelter. "She was the whole reason that I went to the EAU. She bought the pregnancy test for me and it was positive and she was like, 'I'm going to help you pack. You should go.'" Anita's immediate goal was to regain custody of her children and she knew that one of the conditions for getting them back was adequate housing. She knew that she needed help and this time, she did not have alternative housing options such as Chris's place. Without other family or friends to support her, Anita entered New York City's shelter system.

"I just couldn't cope with living [at my grandmother's house] anymore. All of my kids' stuff was still there and I wasn't going anywhere. I would just be sitting on my ass. I had to get out of there. I had to do something or go somewhere. I had to be around people or talk to somebody. Maybe they can help me—not just give me a place to stay but try to hook me up with some kind of counseling…"

Waiting at the EAU

Anita was barely two months pregnant when she applied for shelter at the EAU. While her application only took three days to be approved, her experience at the EAU, however brief, was emotionally draining. "The second night that I was there, I had to sleep there." According to Anita, the EAU waiting room was crowded with mothers and their children. At one point during the evening, Anita moved her legs to stretch and lost the small amount of floor space that she needed to comfortably sleep. "A lot of people would lay blankets out on the floor and [the EAU staff put] little benches against the sides of the walls. I was just sitting up because I wasn't that far along in my pregnancy for people to see that I was actually pregnant." Sometime after midnight, Anita started crying. Unable to control her emotions, she approached EAU staff at the intake desk, pleading to be sent to an overnight placement. "I sat on the floor under the counter—it was the only space I had—and I was crying so they made me go to the psychiatric emergency ward." The hospital held Anita for two hours before releasing her back to the EAU waiting room.

Shelter Life

Today, Anita is a slender, 6-foot tall, 24-year-old woman dressed in a pale pink tank top, pink knit zip-up sweatshirt and matching pink pants. She is clearly in her eighth month of pregnancy, her tummy largely exposed. Her mood often changes, sometimes unexpectedly, and she repeatedly turns silent and downturn after breaking into bouts of spontaneous laughter. While she believes that she is not an outgoing person—"I don't do the concerts, I don't do the boat rides, I don't get into the cars and go to the movies, I don't even go to the fairs like Great Adventures"—she has a sarcastic, witty spark that attracts people. On the other hand, the traumatic experiences of her childhood and young adult life do affect her present way of living and distances potential friends. Anita's past abuse occasionally haunts her with intense sadness or flares up into violent and uncontrollable anger.

This morning, Anita is unusually quiet. "At times, I over-whelm myself with certain things. Like today, I feel depressed. I woke up feeling this way. I don't know why. It just happened. I woke up this morning, crying. Yesterday, I was feeling okay. I was okay yesterday and today I'm not, but I don't let it get the best of me. I don't show too many people how I'm really feeling because they go and write those things down." Doctors disagree whether or not Anita suffers from mental illness. She has been diagnosed with depression, but her current psychiatrist attributes her variable moods and violent outbursts to post-traumatic stress disorder.

Anita is staying at her second shelter placement in the past eight months. She was discharged from another transitional family shelter for disorderly conduct. After catching her neighbor, a fellow shelter resident that she considered a good friend, stealing her CD collection, Anita became so enraged that she began hitting the woman and later, hurting the shelter staff that tried to intervene. "I kicked the door and it opened up and I just went in there and dragged her out. I started wailing on her, up and down the hallway, up and down the hallway. You want to steal? Let me show you what it feels like. Let me show you what happens to people when they steal. I thought you were my friend…"

Anita's longing for friendship and acceptance, as well as her violent reactions to stealing and intrusion of ownership are prominent aspects of her personality. "Everywhere I go, someone wants to take something from me, they want to do something to me." During one of the parenting workshops that she attends, Anita suspected a classmate of stealing her purse. Furious with uncontrollable rage, she found a hammer in a nearby restroom undergoing renovation and chased after her classmate. "I was going to hammer that girl to death because she stole and I don't like when people steal; it's not cool." At her current shelter, Anita has already had arguments and run-ins with some of the residents, but overall, she is happy. She has found a group of friends—mothers like herself who need support and are eager to assist others. "It makes me feel good when I have friends. Well, not really friends but I have people that ... they just like me. They think I'm cool and they want to hang out with me. I don't like to be alone." Anita's moods are changeable but regardless of her temperament, she maintains her humor and signature sarcasm.

Since entering the shelter system, Anita believes she is calmer and more patient now. "I've learned to not let too many things get to me now. Everything is a process. Everything is a process and I'm just one of those little notches waiting to get moved on." Her two priorities are regaining custody of her children and finding an apartment suitable for a family of four. Currently, Claire and Thalia have been in kinship care, living with Anita's great aunt for almost one year, and Anita is eagerly waiting for her ACS court date to find out when or if she will regain custody.

Every two weeks, she spends her Saturday afternoon with Claire, Thalia, and her great-aunt. Her visits are similar to arts and crafts workshops. "I bring washable markers, Barbie crayons, construction paper, scissors, glue sticks, and stickers and I just let them go. They just color and draw and paste and mark up the table. I bring Lysol disinfectant wipes because it gets the stains out really good."

The end of the visit is always the hardest part for Anita. If Claire and Thalia begin acting up—getting upset that they have to leave their mother—the four of them walk over to the nearby K-Mart, visit the "Barbie aisle," and sometimes, in rough situations, she buys her daughters a small toy to momentarily distract them from the larger situation.

Anita has received weekly counseling and therapy sessions at a nearby clinic. She also attends parenting skills workshops run by shelter staff. Occasionally, Anita's past suddenly comes back to haunt her in unexpected ways. For Claire's birthday, she brought special treats to her Saturday foster care visit—a cake and buckets of fried chicken and boxes of pizza. That's when she ran into one of her many "mothers" from the past. "While we were ordering the pizza and stuff, the manager comes up and she's one of my old foster parents. It was a long time ago. She was like, 'You look familiar. Don't I know you from somewhere?' I just said, yeah, I know you."

Anita has been without a home for most of her life. Now, as an adult, she is upset that she is not living independently; however, her experience at the shelter has been a positive one. "A lot of people think that the shelter system is a bad experience or is not the best place to be, but you have to do what you have to do. If it's something that needs to be done in *your* life, you just need to do it."

Two months later, Anita was approved for a Section 8 housing subsidy and immediately moved into a Brooklyn apartment. Shortly after, she received full custody of Claire and Thalia. While Anita says she is doing well emotionally and keeping an upbeat attitude, her family has not steadily received public benefits since leaving the shelter. A mix-up with paperwork on the City's end has left them without an after-care case-worker, and as a result, Anita lacks a formally assigned advocate to deal with the confusion. For now, she has stopped attending therapy and has pulled her children out of daycare in order to save money.

....

In New York City, eighteen percent (18.4%) of homeless parents have children in kinship or foster care and thirty-five percent (35%) have an open case with the Administration for Children's Services (ACS). Out of these cases, nearly eighty percent (79%) are due to neglect, which can cover a wide range of inadequacies in parental care—problems that may have been caused or exacerbated by poverty and homelessness.[4]

Thirty-three percent (33%) of homeless mothers lived apart from their own parents as children, either in kinship care or foster care—over sixteen times the national foster care rate of two percent (2%). Of these, nearly one in five (18.8%) were homeless as children, and nearly two in five (38.9%) experienced violence growing up. This instability in their early life frequently translates into difficulties in adulthood. When compared to the overall homeless population, thirty percent (30%) are more likely to experience addiction disorders; and fifty percent (50%) are more likely to suffer domestic violence and more than twice as likely to be diagnosed with mental illness.[5]

NOTES

1 In 1990, New York's foster care system was under the administration of the Bureau of Child Welfare (BCW). The Administration for Children's Services (ACS) was created in 1996, assuming the BCW's role in overseeing the foster care system.

2 At twenty-four years old, Anita now knows more about her biological father than she did thirteen years ago. Although Anita's father knew that his eleven-year-old daughter was about to be placed in the foster care system, he was young and did not have the resources to adopt her. "He was still living with his mother so why would he come and take me if he couldn't even support himself?" Currently, her father is living with a relative, hiding from the police. Anita does not know the circumstances of the charges against him.

3 Job Corps is a federally funded residential, education, and job-training program for at-risk youth ages sixteen through twenty-four. There are seven Job Corps centers scattered throughout New York State.

4 Ralph da Costa Nunez, *The New Poverty*, (New York City: Insight Books, 1992) 138.

5 Institute for Children and Poverty, "Homelessness: The Foster Care Connection," April 1997: 1.

CHAPTER THREE
Lynn, age 39

Domestic Abuse

He knows that I had cats and I would leave the window open. He climbed through, called the storage company and took every piece of furniture out of my apartment. I came home and was like, "What happened?"

It took me two months to find the storage place that he put my furniture in and I found out that they just sold everything. I lost baby pictures, birth certificates, everything. I basically had nothing left.

When Coby served Lynn divorce papers three years ago, she never expected that he would continue harassing her. After seven years of marriage, Lynn thought that Coby's paranoia, violence, and obsessive tendencies were somewhat predictable. She never thought that he would resort to such a drastic and imaginative scheme. "It kills me to know that I was caught off guard. How could I not think of that? I told him that I'm not coming back. You gave me the papers. I signed them. It's over. Divorce—that's final. But he just figured, 'I'll take your stuff. You got to come back to me.'"

Early Life

As a child, Lynn never expected that at thirty-nine years old, she would be living in a New York City homeless shelter. In fact, good luck seemed to be on Lynn's side since she was an infant. When she and her twin sister were born in Baltimore, Maryland, their biological mother had already given birth to fourteen sons and daughters. Lynn's mother abandoned her and twin sister Kai in the hospital soon after the delivery. "My mother had been very busy, I guess, and twins came along. She couldn't handle twins." By coincidence, the hospital's head nurse's sister had baby twin boys that had recently and unexpectedly passed away. The head nurse alerted her sister about the abandoned twins, and they decided to adopt. "It's a nice little story and [Kai and I] stayed together. I'm glad that they kept us together. I guess my parents were ready for it being that they had twin boys previously. And my aunt was ready to help them out."

Today, Kai has met two of their fourteen siblings; however, Lynn has no interest in meeting her biological family. "Me personally, I don't go looking. To me, I'll leave well enough alone. If we come to meet, then we come to meet. But as far as trying to find them, it's not in my mind to do that."

At age nine, Lynn's family moved from Baltimore, Maryland to Queens, New York, where her parents have since lived. Growing up, Lynn describes her and her sister as "latch-key kids." Both parents worked—her father worked for the Long Island Railroad and her mother was a home—aid at a group home for at-risk boys. As part of her work, their mother would stay at the group home for months at a time. "She had a time-consuming job so most times, we didn't really see her ... It was usually just my father, my sister, and me and we loved it, especially because my mother liked to nit-pick a lot. With their father also gone long hours, Lynn and Kai were often home alone.

"We came home and cooked our own dinner and stuff like that … we did our homework and on the weekends, we had our freedom."

While Lynn views her childhood as generally positive, she remembers one incident between her parents that was particularly painful for the family. "In the middle of their marriage, my father did cheat and it hurt everybody, but we stuck it out. They worked through it." At twelve years old, Lynn and Kai routinely went to the neighborhood bowling alley with their father. One evening, Lynn's father asked the girls not to come with him. Later, after their mother had returned from work, Lynn, her sister, and mother decided to go to the bowling alley. "She got us dressed up and we said, 'Oh yeah! We're going to the bowling alley!' We ran up to our father: 'Hi Dad!'

He said, 'What are you doing here?'

'Mom brought us!' We were standing right next to [his mistress] and didn't even know! … It was sad because that's my father and I love him dearly and it hurt me." Because it happened during Lynn and Kai's summer vacation, their parents sent them to stay with their aunt for the remainder of the break. Lynn's parents used this time to work on repairing their relationship. Looking back, Lynn is better able to understand why her father cheated, considering that her mother was gone so often and for such long periods of time. "As I got older, I could see [why he cheated]. I don't approve of it but I could see why. Tend to forgive and forget. Plus, our allowance went up after that. My father was awfully nice. I guess we knew to play on the guilt thing because my mother also felt bad because she wasn't home."

Motherhood and Work

Throughout high school, Lynn was not as preoccupied by boys or dating as many girls her age. "I didn't date in high school. I was into sports and everything, and I wasn't thinking about guys. Boys were not worth my time." However, soon after graduating from high school, she met Eddie, her first love. "He had just come back from the Navy and that uniform thing—God, he looked good in that! After high school, I saw him and just started dating."

After nearly a year, nineteen-year-old Lynn discovered that she was pregnant. "One thing turned into another and I'm not proud of it, but hey, I love my son. We were going to get married but everything started happening." Lynn discovered that Eddie was involved with drugs. Eddie's father had recently died of a drug overdose and Lynn was shocked and hurt that he would "follow in his father's footsteps." As Eddie's life deteriorated into a routine of heavy drug use, Lynn began to distance herself from him. "It was terrible to see him go through that much pain at that time." Despite her desire to stand by him, Lynn knew that their relationship was over and her pregnancy came first. After giving birth to their son Steven, Eddie visited one time. "My son really never got to know his father. He saw him one time and by then, he was into [drugs] and so I didn't want him near him anyway." Later, Lynn heard that Eddie had died of a drug overdose, just as his own father had died. "It was very disappointing to know that he died the same way. It hurt me and it took me a long time to get back into that mode of dating and seeing people again."

After the tragedy, Lynn's parents, concerned about her fragile emotional state and her ability to raise Steven, insisted that she continue living with them. "It wasn't like I was going to lose sleep or hurt myself—I don't believe in that. It wasn't like I was happy about it but life goes on. I moved on and I talked to [Eddie's] mother. We agreed to everything, that this is the way it's going to be."

Lynn and her parents shared the responsibilities of raising Steven and after about a year, she starting looking for work. Remembering a childhood experience volunteering with the local police department, Lynn decided to apply for work in the areas of corrections and police. "[Kai and I] would do the 109 Precinct Auxiliary and they used to call my sister and I "Cagney and Lacy" because we just were so gung ho. I always wanted a uniform. I was proud to wear it and I wanted to get into that." Lynn applied to both the New York City Department of Corrections and the New York City Police Department; Corrections was the first to offer her a position as an officer for one of the city's women's prisons.

During her year and a half working at the women's jail, Lynn says that her "personality just changed." Relatively sheltered growing up, she believes that the stark contrast of prison life was too overwhelming. "When I got in there, there were things that just made me cry because I had never even seen half of that stuff. It's like a whole new world." In addition to the fairly frequent suicides, violent riots, and intense personalities, she dealt with "heads getting cracked open and officers who would be just as rotten as the inmates." After working at the women's prison for about a year, Lynn began regularly experiencing stress-induced migraines. She felt distanced from Steven, spending the majority of her waking life at work rather than at home. "There was one point where one month, every day I worked overtime.

After that, they saw that I was losing it because I was begging for over-time. They said, 'you have to take some days off'…I didn't think that [my son] recognized me by that point."

Work was not only emotionally difficult for Lynn but it was also physically dangerous. Within a year and a half, she had fractured her wrist and a rib bone during riots among inmates. When Lynn broke her wrist a second time, she knew that she had to make a career change. "I had an inmate that I was holding who they were trying to take out and they jumped her with me holding her and my hand went down with her. I said, 'That's it. I can't take it no more. I'm going to get my education so I don't have to be with you crazy people.'"

Lynn's friend came across a small, quiet college in a rural area of Florida and sent her a promotional videotape of the school. "She said, you got to see this and I was like, I'm going to Florida. It was an 'end-quotes' thing. I just packed up and left. I didn't know nobody down there." After the stressful and emotionally draining experience working for corrections, Lynn chose Florida because it was so differ-ent from the environment in New York. "When you are in New York for all of your life and you have the opportunity, I went. I just jumped for it and the school was nice and small. It wasn't huge where I would get all stressed out."

She took Steven with her for the first few months of school but the living arrangements soon proved difficult. Five-year-old Steven needed a more structured environment and more attention for his chronic asthma. Lynn's parents were more than willing to take care of him while she went to school. So, before her first term ended, she sent Steven back to New York to live with his grandparents. "It was hard, but I knew he was safe. I knew he was being taken care of." Lynn kept in constant contact with Steven by phone and returned to New York during semester breaks.

The price of obtaining her college education was missing out on much of Steven's childhood. Lynn remembers one particular incident that made her realize the little boy she left with her parents was fast becoming a young man. Steven was nearly eight years old when Lynn, in her final semester at school, had come up for the winter holiday. "I went into the bathroom with him—he was my son; he was just a kid. I wasn't looking at him or anything but he actually said, 'Mom, you can't come in here no more.'

I'm like, 'Why not?'

He said, 'Because, I'm a man now.'

I was like, 'You're seven years old. What do you mean you're a man now?'

'Because I got hair.'

'What?'

'I got hair—down there.'

'What?'

'I got hair—down there!'

'Meanwhile, my mom, dad, sister, and grandparents are sitting in the dining room area and they're laughing." When Lynn questioned Steven once more, he flashed his mom to prove that he was, in fact, a man now. "I went, 'Oh.' I opened the door, walked out of the bathroom. My parents were sitting there and I said, 'he got hair down there. I can't go in there no more.'"

Even though Lynn missed out on much of Steven's young life,

she was determined to get a college education. Using student loans and working part-time as head resident adviser in the dormitories, she was able to pay her own way through school. According to Lynn, working as an RA was easy compared to her previous job. "Being that I had experience with corrections, I got things done there!" In addition to work and school, she hosted a show on the college radio. After three years at Florida, Lynn graduated with an associate's degree in broadcast and communications. She immediately moved back to New York to live with her parents and to resume her responsibility of raising Steven, now eight years old.

Returning to New York

Once in New York City, Lynn found an apartment in Queens near her parents' place. Steven still spent most days at his grandparents' apartment but it was not uncommon for him to stay with his mother on weekends or occasional weeknights. In Lynn's view, sharing parenting responsibilities worked out for the best for Steven. "He had the best of both worlds. These types of situations usually don't work out because the grandparents want to take the complete role but that didn't happen and I really thank God for that. My mother and I may have a different view, but when it comes to my son, we both raised him."

Unable to find a job related to her degree in broadcast and communications, Lynn worked for a security firm doing undercover work in the area of employee theft. "So ok, I was a snitch! I was an employee [at a company] but I was there to spy on the other employees. So if I was working at your company and I see you taking something, you won't be there next week." Every week Lynn was sent to a different company or retail store to spy on the employees. While the work was fairly regular, with Lynn often working forty-hour weeks, it was not necessarily reliable. "As long as I got hired and people needed me, I was there." She complemented her security job with occasional part-time work with a talent and promotions company.

Soon after moving back to New York City, Lynn met Mario, a young Italian man and her first love interest since Eddie. "We just saw each other. It was on the Long Island Railroad train station. I was going somewhere with my father and [Mario] seemed to think that I was there everyday. About three weeks later, I went back and he was there. He said, 'I've been here every day waiting to see you.'" Lynn and Mario dated for nearly two years, on and off, before Lynn discovered she was pregnant. "[The relationship] was a back and forth thing because he had to go back and forth between Italy and the United States. Finally, his grandmother died and he wanted me to go there but I said, no. My son is here and I can't go."

Compared to her first pregnancy nine years earlier, Lynn's second pregnancy was difficult. Midway into her term, she became ill and had to leave her security job and part-time work. "I was very sick and I couldn't keep working. I needed help and I got help, really quick." Lynn could not afford her rent payments and on the advice of a friend, went to the Emergency Assistance Unit (EAU) in Manhattan.[1] Within a couple of hours, she was approved for a Section 8 rent subsidy and had found another apartment near her parents in Queens. Some people may wonder why she did not turn to her parents for a temporary place to live instead of going to the EAU for rent help. In her view, this would have been only be putting off the inevitable.

When she gave birth to Patty, Mario came back to visit her. Today, Lynn and Mario continue to keep in touch, but Patty has not seen her father since that initial visit. "Someday, I want to save up money and have her go visit her father. I know where he is and I know that he also got married. Patty's got seven brothers and sisters!"

Soon after Patty was born, Lynn had to find another place to live. After nearly nine months of renting her Section 8 apartment, she was notified that the bank had foreclosed on the building. "The landlord wasn't paying the mortgage and [the tenants] had no idea. We were paying the rent and then we found out that the water bill hadn't been paid in two years. It was just wild." With her Section 8 subsidy, Lynn was able to quickly find another affordable apartment close to her parents and to Steven. She would live in this apartment for the next ten years.

Married Life

When Patty was old enough to go to her grandparents' house, Lynn resumed her part-time job with the security company and occasionally worked for the promotions company. Although she took the parental responsibility of raising Patty, ten-year-old Steven continued living with his grandparents, at least during the week. "I felt that he should be stable. He was used to that school and he stayed stable there."

Nearly a year after giving birth to Patty, Lynn met Coby. He was a sales associate at an electronics store and supplemented his small salary with part-time work at a Manhattan perfume shop. "I would always go into [the perfume store] and say, do you have Taboo? If you want me to keep coming in here, you got to order Taboo. He actually found out where I was working and sent it over, with a rose. I was like, oh man; it was embarrassing." Lynn and Coby steadily dated for the next two years. Because of her past relationships, dates with Coby were filled with conversation rather than physical intimacy. "We just talked and I felt if you could have a conversation with somebody, you got to love them. We fell in love and got married." They had a small city-hall wedding and Coby moved into Lynn's apartment, assuming a paternal role for Patty. Slightly over a year after their marriage, Lynn discovered she was pregnant with her second daughter, Priscilla.

For the next five years, married life was simple and quiet. Lynn quit her jobs with security and promotions to work as a stay-at-home mother, occasionally babysitting to make extra money. Coby began full-time work with the electronics store, still in his sales associate position. Lynn, Coby, Patty, and Priscilla lived as a family, with Steven alternating between his grandparents' place and his mother's apartment.

A Change in Coby

In their sixth year of marriage, Coby's father suffered a stroke, debilitating many of his cognitive functions. Because his father lived outside the country, Coby could not afford to visit him as often as desired. "His father was very sick and I could see that he was very depressed. He started drinking and started hanging out with the wrong people...He just went off the deep end." Coby became reliant

and she was impressed by his sudden motivation for self-improvement. However, after the first few weeks, Lynn discovered that he had been lying—Coby had never attended a meeting. When Lynn confronted him, he refused to admit his guilt and immediately began blaming others. "He said, 'The supervisor's lying.' 'Why would a supervisor lie? What is the purpose for him to lie to me?' He said, 'You must be having an affair with him.' I said, 'That's it. Good-bye.'"

The deterioration of Lynn and Coby's marriage has been difficult for Patty and Priscilla. While Patty stays away from him, Priscilla is still young and has mixed feelings towards her father. "The little one is just crazy about him but she knows that he's doing wrong. She loves her father but she won't go near him also because she knows what he's doing. Sometimes we'll see him in Queens and she'll say, 'Mom, there he is.' I'll say, 'Oh God, let's duck.' I hated to do that and she wanted so much to see him but she knew I couldn't be around. It had to be a neutral person to have her see him."

Eighteen-year-old Steven is the only family member who does not have the slightest mixed emotions about Coby. Whenever he hears about Coby's harassment, Steven feels the need to physically attack him. "My son is just like, 'give me the word; give me the word.'" After sophomore year of high school, Steven left school due to academic difficulties. He continued living at his grandparents' house for the next two years before enrolling in New York State's job corps program, an alternative residential high school program for at-risk-youth in upstate New York. Living at his grandparents' house and later, the job corps center, Steven has remained slightly distanced from the family during most of Coby's harassment.

Coby Turns to ACS

Two years after their divorce, Coby's possessiveness had escalated even more. Even though Lynn had not been in a relationship since the divorce, he had become increasingly jealous and paranoid, and he was convinced that she had a number of male companions. Lynn felt unsafe in her own neighborhood and suspected that Coby's friends regularly informed him about her and her daughters' whereabouts. "They would be looking, watching my movements so it was like, every time that I turned around, he would know my business." More upsetting than Coby's friends was Coby himself. "He kept calling, ringing the bell, standing on the corner, [and] looking out through the back of the window. I felt like I was in one of those Lifetime movies." Because he was not physically harming Lynn, the most she could do was file an order of protection with the police. Lynn felt helpless.

Today, Lynn has an open ACS (Administration for Children's Services) case for Patty and Priscilla, which she blames Coby for filing. The incident happened over one year ago during summer break, and she was working for the local elementary school as a peer mediator. "I was going to get test grids for the kids and this nice young fellow had a car. He ran me over there, I jumped out, and jumped back into the car. [Coby] saw me getting into the car and thought that young stud was my new [boyfriend]. So he called up ACS and said that I sold my kids for a thousand dollars worth of cocaine! A thousand, at that! Just a thousand!" Lynn says that ACS took Patty and Priscilla away a few days later; it was an overnight removal that was solely based on Coby's accusations.

By this point, Lynn was full of anger and was convinced that she would physically harm him, even kill him, if given the chance. "I am not going to lie. I would have killed him in a minute if he came near me. I am not going to lie. I was really, totally angry." In court, Coby retracted his accusations; however, Lynn could not contain her emotions in front of the judge. "I actually threatened him. Yes! I threatened him with the judge there and they said, 'you have anger management problems.' Well yes! Look what I'm dealing with! It was the worse thing that he did in my life." Due to her in-court outburst, Lynn's ACS case is still open for court-supervision purposes.

A Forced Move

Nearly three years after their divorce, Coby's irrational jealously and possessiveness was still continuing. "I had to disconnect the phone three times and he always found out the new number. Then I got a cell phone and he started calling me at the school." Lynn felt pressure to quit her job as a peer mediator, but with no financial backups she was hesitant to do so. When Coby turned violent against her coworkers, she knew she had to leave. "He was stalking me. He went through and started beating up the males. I just had to leave because it didn't make sense. These were my friends. I worked with these people for three years and I couldn't have him ... I mean, he already knocked out a tooth of one of my friends and he was just helping me carry my bags."

Lynn, now unemployed, relied on her modest savings to support her family. Her occasional work with the promotions company was no longer an option; the 9-11 tragedy had shut down the company. She soon realized she could not pay the rent and was forced to leave her apartment of nearly ten years. The family moved in with a friend, and Lynn planned to keep their belongings in a rented storage space while she considered more permanent options.

Before Lynn had fully moved out of the apartment, Coby shocked her for the final time. Sneaking into her apartment one afternoon, Coby moved all of the family's furniture and valuables into a rented storage space. Lynn believes that this was his attempt to re-establish her dependence on him; she would need his help in order to find and regain ownership of her assets. Even after Coby took all of her furniture, Lynn did not contact him. Instead, she called every storage company in the New York metropolitan area until she found the one holding her belongings. It had been tricky—there are many storage companies in the area and Coby had slightly misspelled her name. It took her two months to find the right place. During that time, the storage company had auctioned off the family's furniture, throwing away all papers stored in the drawers, including birth certificates, diplomas, letters, and pictures. "They sold everything that was of value and the rest, they just threw out so they didn't even bother to look. They took what they wanted and threw out the rest."

Last Resorts

For the next two months, Lynn used the family's savings to rent rooms from friends, doubling up in their already overcrowded apartments. For Lynn, it was very important that her daughters remain near their old neighborhood and attend the same schools, thus limiting their housing options. "Education is so important to me with my girls and I wanted them to stay focused." Lynn, Patty, and Priscilla first stayed with a family friend, spending the night in sleeping bags on the floor. After a few weeks, it was apparent that the apartment was too small for three extra additions and the family soon moved to another friend's apartment. "There was just no room and I don't like going up on people."

In the new place, the family had a twin bed and two sleeping bags, and private space made the accommodations more bearable. However, Coby's possessiveness and unpredictable violence soon became a problem for their hosts. "He was getting to the point where he would show up and punch somebody out, and I'm like, I just can't do this to these people. They are nice. They're my friends and if I really care for them, I can't have him punching out people because he thinks that I'm having an affair with them." Soon after Lynn's family moved in, her friend's husband suffered a stroke. Lynn believes that he had become overly stressed from the crowded living situation and the potential for a violent confrontation with Coby. "When he had the stroke, I was like, that's it. My problem is becoming your problem now. That was the last straw and I realized that this is it."

Turning towards Help

According to Lynn, Coby's harassment, stealing, and unpredictable behavior forced her to turn to the EAU. "It was the last place that I wanted to go to, but I had no choice. I didn't want to go to my relatives because most of them are all over the state and I don't know what his thinking is about. I don't want to jeopardize anyone." She knew that her family could no longer survive without help, but she did not want to endanger her parents and other relatives by staying with them. Lynn turned to her former public assistance center and they gave her directions to the EAU in the Bronx.

With less than ten dollars left in savings, Lynn's family arrived at the EAU on an early Sunday morning in mid April. Compared to her first and relatively easy experience over ten years ago with Emergency Assistance Units, she found this new EAU very different. "They call it 'central booking' around here because it's like you went to prison—that's the way that it felt. The people there were so rude." Lynn still vividly remembers their five days waiting at the EAU for a shelter placement. "The traveling was the hardest part. You are bringing bags and nobody tells you that each night, you have to carry them back and forth, back and forth...I had a little bit but there were people there with TVs and lots of bags and suitcases and they came with the illusion that they were going to get placed right then and on that day. They didn't know that they were going to get shuttled back and forth for overnights."

In addition to the exhaustion of traveling between overnight hotel placements and the EAU, she remembers the pervasiveness of filth, drugs, and sickness as being particularly difficult to endure. "We had to put bags up on places because rats and mice were coming up and roaches were all over the place." According to Lynn, the EAU restrooms tended to be drug-infested hotspots. "I was so scared to let my daughters use the bathrooms. We would go to the ones where the guards were standing because other ones, where the guards were not standing, you got people in the bathroom shooting up—shooting and sniffing." Lynn met families with pink eye and children with chicken pox or food poisoning, sick from the EAU's food. "There were quite a few [people] who were throwing up and dehydrated just because of the food."

After five days of waiting at the EAU, Lynn and her two daughters were placed in a shelter, or "family center," in Harlem. The night that they moved into their new residence, Priscilla came down with a serious bout of food poisoning caused by the family's last dinner at the EAU. "My youngest daughter got very sick … we got placed that night and at the family center, they told me that the hospital was just a couple of blocks down. I took her there and they hospitalized her for a couple of days." After two days in the hospital, Priscilla was able to return to the shelter. Today, Lynn is able to joke about the EAU's shocking conditions: "Horror Story: EAU! Come to the EAU! You'll never come out alive!"

Isolated but Safe

When a room opened up at a shelter in the Bronx, Lynn was transferred. Although moving was another transition for the family, this new shelter offered more supportive services than the center in Harlem, and she was somewhat glad to be living in the Bronx. Lynn was sure that her family and friends, and especially Coby, would never imagine her living in the Bronx. "I was like, he [will] never figure this one out because I've never been to the Bronx except to go to the Bronx zoo. But to *live* in the Bronx!"

To this day, Lynn has not told her friends, parents, or relatives any specifics about her situation. She is afraid to tell her mother about her family's location for fear that Coby will find them. "I call my mother and say, 'I'm fine. I'll talk to you later.' I try to keep it short because the less that she knows, she can't say anything ... I tell [my son] that everything's all right, that I'm fine, and if anyone's looking for me, just tell them that I'm fine ... I feel that the safest bet is not to tell my friends where I'm at because somebody might know them that knows him. You know, it's hard. I don't have none of my good friends here and I can't talk to anybody." Lynn says that Patty and Priscilla have been her greatest support, enabling her to keep going and stay positive. "They keep me well entertained; they keep me laughing. Why we aren't in California getting rich somewhere with all of this funniness in the family, I don't know!"

While Lynn has been able to maintain her humor about the situation, the process of getting approved for a new apartment has been particularly difficult for her family. Families in the shelter system need to have an active public assistance case in order to move into permanent housing. This condition applies to all families, regardless if they are employed or have other sources of income, since the act of receiving shelter is considered a form of public assistance. Although Lynn had received public assistance in the past, her case information had not been properly entered in the city's database and she needed to resubmit certain documents, such as her family's birth certificates. In order to apply for housing, she needed to resolve her PA situation by ordering official copies of the family's birth certificates, costing thirty dollars a piece. With less than ten dollars to her name, Lynn was frustrated and did not know how she was going to get new birth certificates for the family. "[The PA workers] can punch up the old number that I had and I'm there so I'm like, what's the problem? I had to have all of that stuff to get on it then but they're saying, we need it now. But if I don't have the money to get the birth certificates, how am I supposed to get it?"

After nearly four months since they applied for shelter at the EAU, Catholic Charities donated the money needed to order the birth certificates; thankfully, Lynn's family is now receiving public assistance benefits. Lynn has also found a job training program, which will prepare her to earn a food handler's license for a career in catering. Cooking and baking have become therapeutic exercises and she looks forward to working in the food industry, possibly starting her own small family bakery.

Since entering the shelter system, Lynn has not heard any news about Coby. "I haven't heard anything and I'm not asking. I feel like, don't talk him up and don't go asking anybody about where he is. I don't want to talk him up because you never know what he's thinking or what he might do. I haven't heard nothing. For all I know, he might be in jail or he might have decided to give it up. But I don't want to contact his sister or anything to find out because it's like talking him up. Just leave it alone." Although Lynn had previously somewhat sympathized with Coby, thinking his father's illness was perpetuating his continued downfall into alcohol and paranoia, she no longer empathizes with his situation. "It started with the father but now it's an excuse. I mean, I could start drinking and everything for the place that I'm in, but it's an excuse."

Lynn tries to keep an open mind when considering her options for leaving the shelter system. While she hopes to secure employment before making any big changes, she is thinking about moving out-of-state and commuting to work in New York. "I'm hoping that with Section 8, we can go somewhere else and commute back and forth. Even if I go to Maryland, I could at least commute back and forth with the Amtrak to New York. It's about three hours. I have a great-aunt [in Maryland] and she will watch [Patty and Priscilla] while I go back and forth to work." When asked why she wants to relocate, she responds, "I don't know, I feel like New York's just pushing us out."

At thirty-nine years old and struggling to start her life over again, Lynn knows she is in a difficult and often discouraging place; however she tries to look towards the future rather than linger over the past. "I can't get no lower than this. Right about now, I don't think that I can get no lower than this. I let my kids know, hey, you can only go up."

Three months later, Lynn and her family found a one-bedroom apartment in Washington Heights, far from their former Queens neighborhood. Around this time, she started the job training and internship program, in preparation to earn her food handler's license. Out of the twenty-three people who started the program, Lynn was among the eight to graduate. She now works a full time internship, baking breads, muffins, and pies for a large daycare facility. Both Patty and Priscilla attend school nearby, and after work, Lynn and her daughters walk home to their new apartment.

....

Domestic abuse is the most commonly cited reason for family homelessness throughout the country.[2] In New York, roughly half (47%) of homeless families have histories of abuse and one in four (25%) cite it as their primary reason for seeking shelter.[3]

Children who have witnessed or experienced abuse are more likely to suffer from emotional distress and physical illness since becoming homeless. They often experience serious neglect, as battered mothers are many times depressed, traumatized, or emotionally unavailable while trying to cope with their own situations. Further, these children are far more likely to become victims or abusers as adults compared to those who grow up without abuse in the home, thus passing the cycle of violence and victimization to a new generation.[4]

NOTES

1 Until the mid 1990s, there were EAUs in Brooklyn, Queens, Manhattan, and the Bronx. In 1993, the Queens EAU shut its doors and by the end of 1994, both Brooklyn and Manhattan locations had also closed.

2 Institute for Children and Poverty, "Day to Day...Parent to Child: The Future of Violence Among Homeless Children in America," (January 1998), 2.

3 Ralph da Costa Nunez, *A Shelter is Not a Home... Or Is It?* New York: White Tiger Press, 2004, 77.

4 Day to Day 3.

CHAPTER FOUR
Denise, age 42

Addiction Disorders

I felt like I was in a maze. I was trying to get out and I would almost get to the exit, but something would pull me to the side, I would go the wrong way, and I would start using drugs again. It just seemed like I could never get out. I used to pray to God, "Help me get out of this maze. Once I get out, I'm going to stay out!"

Denise has temporarily stopped using drugs in the past; however, this is the first time she has been clean for longer than a year. At forty-two years old, she has spent over half of her life as a drug addict: sniffing coke, smoking crack, and floating between jails, strangers' houses, and abusive relationships. Denise has been clean for eighteen months and she believes that rather than starting her life over, she is starting a new chapter in a previously turbulent book. She intentionally remains very aware of her recently troubled past. "[My mother] says that was then and this is now, don't dwell on things in the past. But I have to think about where I've been and what I've done so I can think about where I'm going. I don't want to go back there."

A New Home

Denise was eight years old when she moved to New York from Georgia with her mother and three brothers. After experiencing years of verbal abuse and physical violence, Denise's mother decided to leave her alcoholic husband and make a new life for herself and her children. "My mother just got tired of the abuse and she left. She gathered her stuff, got on a bus, and came to New York." Even though Denise's mother already had four children when she restarted her life in New York, she was still young. By age fifteen, her mother had married and was pregnant with her first child. Before she turned twenty, she had given birth to two sons and was pregnant with Denise, her third child and only daughter.

After leaving Georgia, Denise spent the rest of her childhood in Westbury, Long Island in an apartment next door to her grandmother and great-grandmother's house. Her grandmother took an active role in raising the family; however, her mother still held the reigns in the household. Denise remembers her mother as a harsh disciplinarian but emphasizes that her mother's punishments were never "abusive." "My mother beat us when we were kids but she really didn't kill us or anything. She didn't go extreme…[Overall] I had a pretty decent childhood. My mom made sure that we were taken care of and we got the things that we needed. We survived without having a father."

Meeting Anthony

At fourteen years old, Denise was introduced to Anthony. "He was sixteen and he had a gleam in his eye. We talked and kind of got together. I was with him for seventeen years." Looking back, Denise believes that she started everything too early—her relationship with Anthony, her experimentation with marijuana, and her longing to

grow up and hang out with the older girls. "I started smoking cigarettes at a young age and I wanted to drink and I wanted to hang out.
Instead of being a teenager and just growing, I wanted to do everything *fast*."

Even though she associated with an older crowd of girls and
began a serious relationship with Anthony, Denise was careful to graduate from high school and to avoid an early pregnancy. "My mother
always told me, 'I want you to finish school with no strings attached.'"
When Denise first heard this, she did not know what her mother was
referring to. She thought, "Something's going to be attached to me?
What is it? I don't know what she's talking about but I don't want it
attached to me! Then, [my mother] told me: no babies, no problems."

Denise's mother did not finish high school due to her own
early pregnancies, and Denise took special care to listen to her mother's advice. "She was always pushing us: "I want you to have a better
life than what I had. I never finished school but I want you guys to
finish school." Her mother's prodding paid off; Denise and her three
brothers all have high school diplomas. Although she made sure that
she graduated, she never spent much time on school work and teach-
ers often mentioned that she was not reaching her full academic
potential. "I was the low-key type of student, just in the background
doing my work and that's it; nothing extra added." Throughout her
last year in high school, she attended classes during the morning and
left school during the afternoon. "When they told me that you only
need a half a day of school—you only need x-amount of credits—to
graduate, well, that was it. I could have taken extra credits or did
something else, but for the whole year of twelfth grade, I was leaving

and going home at noon or earlier. I would stay with my friends for lunch and then I would just cut out."

Moving Around

Soon after finishing high school, Denise attended classes for a cosmetology degree and worked part-time at a stationery store while living at her family's apartment in Long Island. Living at home was not a free ride. In order to teach Denise financial responsibility, her mother charged her a weekly rent for room and board. "It was fifty dollars per week and if I didn't pay one week, then I would have to pay double the next week—she made sure of that. But she helped me out in the long run when I left and I finally moved out." Her mother had saved a portion of each week's rent and using the accumulated rent payments, Denise was able to pay the required security deposit and one month's rent when she moved into her own place, a rented room in an apartment leased by someone else.

Twenty-two-year-old Denise moved into an apartment around the corner from Anthony's family's place in Hempstead, Long Island. After living there for six months, she moved in with Anthony and his family. Although they had been continuously dating for the past eight years, Denise and Anthony's relationship was rocky. Even when their relationship was in a good place, Anthony was not always monogamous. Moreover, Denise felt uncomfortable around his friends and believed he placed his male friends before their relationship. "I couldn't really talk to him, express my feelings to him, and tell him how I really felt about what was going on—I couldn't. And his friends, I just didn't feel like I fit in with them. I felt uncomfortable at gatherings that he had and so I said, 'I'll have a drink.' I strayed away and that's how I started doing drugs. The people I started hanging out with, they were doing it so I said, 'Ok, I'll try it.' It made me feel good at that time. It made me forget about what was going on around me. They made me feel more comfortable and I just did it to fit in."

Denise finished her coursework and earned a temporary cosmetology license. By this time, she had started doing drugs on a regular basis. Working off the books at a hair salon, she began receiving public assistance to supplement her income. "I was getting their money and my money so I had more money to buy more drugs—it was stupid." After her temporary license expired, Denise had no motivation and was "too distracted" by the drugs to pass the required state board exam to get her permanent license. "I was doing a lot of coke, *a lot* of coke. I was more obsessed with coke than I was smoking crack. I just felt like I had to have that stuff." With her increased drug use, the relationship quickly deteriorated; Anthony disapproved of her lifestyle and although he continually pressured her to get help, Denise felt that he still put friends, work, and flirtations before her needs.

At twenty-seven years old, while still living with Anthony's family, Denise discovered she was pregnant. "I was doing so many drugs that I didn't really know." During the first few months of her pregnancy, she witnessed the effects of crack on an infant's health and finally stopped using drugs. "My girlfriend's baby, he couldn't walk or talk; he was bad. She went full term and he was only about two pounds. He was so black, black from all of the smoke—he was a tar baby." With her relationship with Anthony still uncertain and in order to get help with the pregnancy, Denise moved back to her mother's apartment and continued to live there after the birth of her first son Nick. Miraculously, Nick was a healthy baby and did not suffer from cocaine withdrawal.

After a year of living at home and raising Nick, Denise moved back with Anthony and his family. Still trying to hold together the semblance of a normal family life, she found work as a cashier at a home and garden store and continued to play the role of wife and mother. "I was dipping and dabbing here and there; I was trying to work, take care of my family, and hang out at the same time. I was working still and dressing—looking nice—and you wouldn't even think it would be me. But on the weekends, I'd get paid and go hang out and sniff."

Dependent on Anthony's family's apartment and his straggling income as a musician, Denise knew the limits of her resources. During the particularly bad points in their relationship, she attempted to leave Anthony by turning to the New York City shelter system. "People told me about the EAU.[1] They were telling me to just go there and get an apartment. They were saying that you need to get out of here and go down there, but it's on you." Denise took two-year-old Nick to the EAU. "They gave us food, blankets, everything. I was going to go to a place that night but it was almost two in the morning. I was so scared—I was really freaking out—and I called Anthony and he talked me into coming back home."

Shortly after, when Denise and Anthony temporarily put their relationship on hold, she turned to a seven-day residential treatment center to avoid homelessness. "I signed myself in because I was hanging out on the street and scared to go home to my mother. I kept thinking, 'What am I going to tell my mother.' I called her and told her that I needed some help, I needed to go and clean myself. She knew what I was doing anyway." At the time, her mother took care of Nick, and Denise returned to her mother's house when the program finished. She remained clean for two or three months until she decided to move in with Anthony again.

At thirty years old, Denise moved into a small apartment in Woodside, Queens with Anthony. The difficulties of their relationship quickly returned and she relapsed. "Anthony started leaving me again and going to rehearsal, rehearsal, rehearsal, and then he cheated on me. I strayed away and started getting high all over again. I medicated my feelings." The realization that he was continuing his infidelities pushed her only further into her drug addiction. "Anthony would leave and I'd say, 'Ok. Go. See you later. I've got something to keep me company.' It wasn't good company and now I know that. But at that time, I thought that it was good company because it kept me happy."

For Anthony's part, watching Denise's drug and alcohol addiction worsen over the years frustrated and angered him. He was finally fed up with the drugs and signed her up for Narcotics Anonymous. "I just did it because he said, 'Go to these meetings and you better do this.' But in my heart, I wasn't really trying. I used to do drugs and then go to the meeting or I'd leave from the meeting and couldn't wait to come home because I'd have something waiting for me." Denise remembers the desperation she felt for drugs: "I remember one night

I was pushing my son in a cart, trucking to the Woodside projects to get some crack."

Eventually, she lost her job at the home and garden store and did not look for other employment. As her drug addiction began to consume more and more of daily life, Denise's responsibilities as a mother fell to the sidelines. "I wasn't coming home at night. I was hanging out and missing days of [Nick's] school. They would call Nick's father—'Come pick up your son. We can't reach your wife.'"[2] Denise, embarrassed about the extent of her addiction, resorted to lying to cover up her disease: "the lies, the conniving, the deceit—it was bad."

An Empty Apartment

"I came home one day and the apartment was empty. Anthony moved into another apartment right down the street. I didn't know that at the time but I know now. He left. I just came in and got whatever I could carry and I left."

Anthony had been telling Denise about their financial difficulties and the need to find another apartment, but she had not been listening. Her thirty-two-year-old life had deteriorated into a time-consuming, energy-draining search for money and drugs. After leaving the empty Woodside apartment, Denise wandered between drug addicts' and suppliers' places, staying one or two nights at the various residences. She was too embarrassed to contact her mother. "I was too ashamed. I was beginning to look bad. By then, my skin had started getting messed up and…I started getting skinny, skinny, skinny." In addition to her changed appearance, Denise's thin body started shaking. "They call that the DPs. I was shaking all of the time. Basically, it was when I had too much and I needed rest. I used to rock with my legs and rock, rock, rock; I wasn't even aware that I was doing it."

Denise made money by robbing people and juggling.[3] "I used to rob people. I'd be nice to you, sweet talk you, and then a check would come—social security checks, welfare checks, didn't matter— and we'd hang out with each other." Denise, or "Auntie" as she was known on the streets, eventually began a small prostitution ring. "I was hanging out on the street—they called it the 'stroll'—and these girls started coming up to me. They wanted me to watch their backs and help them when they'd go on dates with these guys. Then they would come back to me and bring me their money. I was the madam and they were my girls. That's how I used to get money: hanging out on the stroll, robbing people, prostitution, all of that."

During this time, Denise lost legal custody of four-year-old Nick. "[Anthony] went to court and he got custody because I never showed up. I never knew he was going to court. I was too busy running around the streets." To Denise, forfeiting her role as a mother was devastating. At first, she tried to keep in contact with Nick through phone conversations but eventually, Anthony asked her to stop calling. "I'd get on the phone and always be crying. I was a mess. Anthony said to me, 'If you can't call here and be calm, please don't call because you're upsetting him. Every time he gets off of the phone he's always crying and upset.' So I stopped calling and that made things even worse. I began drinking more."

You're the One

After three months of bouncing between strangers' houses, Denise met Eric. Eric had his own house, lived off of SSI payments, and had spent most of his sixty-year-old life doing drugs. Although he had found equilibrium, balancing his drug use with everyday tasks, his life still centered around obtaining and using cocaine. According to Denise, "When [Eric] first saw me, he said, 'You're the one.'

'I'm the one what?'

'You're the one that I love.'

From that day on, that was it. We started talking but we didn't get together. We were just friends but he kept telling me that he liked me. For me, it was just some place to go. One night, I needed a place to stay to go to sleep and I ended up falling asleep there. He made me comfortable and I went to sleep; I started staying there."

For the next ten years, Denise lived with Eric and took the brunt of his mood swings, temper flare-ups, and violent behavior. "One minute he was nice and then one minute he was angry. He snapped. I don't understand how he could beat me up and yell and scream at me, and then he could turn around and say, 'Oh, look at the TV. Come here, come here.' There was something seriously wrong with him. Now that I realize it, what was I thinking to stay with him that long? I had so many opportunities to get away. What was I thinking about? But I was secure; I was getting high. That's what kept me there—the drugs, getting high."

"I pretty much did what I pleased: I came when I wanted to, left when I wanted to, slept when I needed to, ate when I needed to. He let me do whatever I wanted to do and in the meantime, he was still doing drugs and he was still abusing me and making me feel like nothing and I settled for that. I took it because at the time, I was happy doing those damn drugs. I accepted it."

Denise is still missing teeth—reminders of Eric's sporadic, but violent, beatings. "He knocked a couple of teeth out. He loosened a tooth and it finally fell out by itself, just fell out by the root...I was always afraid of hitting him back because I thought that there were consequences of what might happen. I was kind of really afraid to hit him."

At the time, Denise did not associate Eric's behavior with domestic violence. "[A friend] used to say, 'You are a victim and don't even know it. She kept telling me, 'You don't even know that you're a victim of domestic violence.' I said, 'Nah, I don't think so.'"

Second Chance at Motherhood

After living with Eric for three years, Denise discovered she was pregnant; Eric was the father. As with her first son, Denise stopped using drugs for the last months of her pregnancy and at thirty-five years old, she gave birth to her second healthy son. As soon as she delivered Kevin, she returned to her normal routine of drinking and heavy drug use. Looking back on her pregnancies, Denise believes she made poor choices regarding her prenatal care. "I thank God that neither [of my sons] came out with drugs in their systems. I went full term, no problems, no complications, and they are healthy, fine—they're both smart. I'm just hoping down the line...I think they'll be all right. I just took things for granted."

Denise and Eric used drugs in the house; however, they usually tried to keep their habit separate from Kevin by sending him to their neighbor Nanna's house. Kevin's visits with Nanna almost always signaled that either Denise or Eric was using drugs at home. Nanna also played a motherly role for Denise. "She used to always talk to me and tell me the things that I wasn't doing right. She was like my mother or my grandmother. Sometimes I would just sit there and cry." While Nanna's willingness to watch and protect Kevin enabled Denise to further her drug habit, Nanna's motherly sternness was her only positive support during that time period. Out of embarrassment about her deteriorated state, she had cut off communication with her mother and brothers.

While Denise believes that she and Eric provided for Kevin's physical needs as an infant and young child, she acknowledges that she was unable to provide for his emotional growth. "We kept a clean house and had food in the house. Kevin had what he needed except for us being there emotionally. Actually, his father was there. It was me, really, that wasn't there. I was there to help him but I didn't really want to be around him. I would talk with him, play with him, but still, I wasn't really there."

Trouble with the Law

Denise was emotionally absent from Kevin, and her bouts in and out of jail occasionally kept her physically apart from him. Most of her numerous arrests have put her in jail for one or two nights. She has pleaded guilty to attempted sale of an illegal substance, prostitution, and criminal trespassing. "They got me twice for [criminal trespassing]. There were buildings that were under surveillance for drug trafficking and they saw me in that building and that's how I got arrested one day. Another time I got arrested for criminal trespassing for a sweep. They had a sweep and I just happened to be coming out of the store and everybody was there; it was bad."

When Kevin was six months old, Denise was arrested for violating probation after she missed a sentencing for a previous offense. "Eric kept saying, 'I know she's going to be there. She's not going to miss this.' And I missed it. I was hanging out and getting high. They put out a warrant for my arrest." She was incarcerated for twenty-one days in Riker's Island. Eric and Nanna watched Kevin. When Denise returned home, she thought, "It seemed like I hadn't seen [Kevin] in forever. Look how big he got! I was freaking out and it was only twenty-one days."

Over the next four years, Denise continued her life with drugs while trying to raise Kevin. She was arrested twice; the most serious charge was for attempted sale of a controlled substance when she bought drugs for a friend's acquaintance. "Me being stupid, I went to get it for him and I came back and just looked around me. I saw that something was not right—a car from here, a car from there, a car over there, two guys walking towards me…I was like, oh God, you just screwed up. You just screwed up! So the drugs that I had in my hand, I took them and swallowed them. But it didn't matter because I had already given the guy the real thing anyway."

Denise pleaded guilty to the felony charge, spent a few nights in jail, and was released on probation. A couple of months passed before she again violated probation. "All I had to do was fill out a questionnaire once a month and take it to the office. Once a month—take it there, get another form, leave. No probation officer, nothing. I was stupid. I was too busy drinking and getting high and I had been arrested already so I thought that they were going to check [for drug use] and I was scared to go. My eyes were all red, I was very skinny, and I just started drinking more. I was just scared to go and they put a bench warrant out for me."[4]

When Denise learned about the bench warrant, she decided to turn herself in. That evening she stayed at a friend's house, smoked crack, and got a good night's sleep. "I got up the next morning and said, 'I'm ready. I'm tired of running; I'm just tired.'" When Denise arrived at the courthouse, she was prepared to go directly to jail, and when the judge sentenced her to Riker's Island, she did not cry. She calmly put her hands behind her back, kissed four-year-old Kevin on the cheek, and left for prison. She was incarcerated for thirty-seven days.

Reaching for Help

During her second week in jail, Denise's lawyer asked if she had a problem with drugs. She responded, "Look at me! Look! I am 109 pounds, soaking wet. Yes, I have a problem with drugs. Yes, I need help." Denise was tired of her life with drugs. She was tired of getting arrested, having problems with the police, settling for an abusive relationship, and being unable to provide for Kevin and Nick. Denise's addiction to crack and coke was also taking a toll on her body. "It messes with your system so bad. It makes your skin color become three shades darker than your normal skin tone. I used to be so dark. My face was ashy all of the time. It also numbs your body to where you can't even eat. That's why you lose so much weight. Your body's so numb that you don't even want to eat."

With the help of her lawyer, Denise entered a twenty-eight day drug treatment program after serving thirty-seven days in jail. When she returned to Eric's house, Denise began attending a city-mandated program that held counseling sessions, tested her urine for drugs, and monitored her progress. But after two months of staying clean, she got high. "I was living with Eric but we weren't together. I hated him. Yeah, I did. I hated him. I went out one night with this other guy and I came home around four o'clock in the morning. I thought Eric would be upset so I decided that if I bought him something, he probably wouldn't bother me. But instead, he got up, opened the door for me and went right back to sleep. The next day, I felt something in my pocket and nobody was home except me. I thought, maybe just this once."

One week later, Denise's counselor confronted her on her drug use. "He said, 'Don't tell me that you're not getting high because I know that you are. It shows in your urine and your urine don't lie. You come in here again, you got until next Tuesday, you're going to lose your son and you're going to go back to jail because I'm going to lock you up. You don't need this! I know you can do this!'" Denise appreciated her counselor's fatherly discipline. She felt that he took a genuine, personal, and active interest in her struggle to stay clean. "When I first went into the program, [the staff] taught me how to do everything and talk about my feelings and this and that but they never really talked to me like they really cared about me. [My counselor] talked to me like he really cared and I still call him up today and I write him Christmas cards."

Denise realized that she had too much to lose by continuing her drug habit. Her counselor enrolled her in a more comprehensive outpatient program that offered various support groups, educational programs, and one-on-one counseling. Since enrolling in the program, she has remained clean.

Leaving Eric

For the six months following her enrollment in the new program, Denise began her struggle to remain drug-free while continuing to live with Eric and raise six-year old Kevin. "Eric would smoke in the house the whole night and sometimes, during the day. I'd get up and go into the bathroom and see a lot of smoke around and the fan would be on. He didn't care." Living with Eric was destructive to Denise's fight to stay clean and hazardous to her physical safety. They constantly fight and Denise knew that she had to leave Eric and find her own apartment. Although her mother offered her apartment for a temporary stay, Denise did not consider it a realistic option. "They offered to change the computer room into a bedroom but I don't want to deal with it. I want my own place and I need the space for my son and me." Denise viewed her mother's house as a temporary solution and instead, tried to consider other more permanent options. As an unemployed single mother still battling a drug addiction, Denise looked to the EAU. "I did hear stories about the EAU. [People] knew about Eric and me fighting all of the time. They said, 'You got to get out of here.' I was thinking, the EAU—oh my God. Just thinking about it was frightening."

While Denise continued to weigh her options for housing, her relationship with Eric continued to deteriorate. One morning, Eric found her private journal. Upset with what Denise was writing about him and their relationship, he became violent. "He beat me up that morning and pulled a knife on me and everything. My son saw it. He told me to get out. I went to the police department and filed a report. Eric got locked up but it didn't stick because I never went to court. I didn't know when to go to court because my papers were going to his house and he told me that he was ripping them up." Eric ended up going to jail for nine days and enrolled in a court-mandated anger management program.

After filing the report at the police station, Denise went to a friend's house for advice. Together, she and her friend called various social service agencies until one organization gave her an address in the Bronx. When she arrived at the flat, windowless, brick building, Denise discovered that it was the EAU. "I asked the lady, 'What is this place?' and she said the EAU. I was like, 'The EAU?!'"

Applying for Shelter

"I have never, ever been to a place like that in all of my life. Oh my God! It was disgusting!…You couldn't even use the bathrooms, you couldn't shower, you couldn't do nothing. There was no place to sit and hardly no place to stand. Someone would move and you would run and steal her seat—it was so bad." Denise had escaped an environment of drugs and alcohol use, but in her view the EAU was not much better. People frequently left the EAU to get high and Denise remembers them returning with bloodshot eyes and hazy looks.

For the first night, Denise and Kevin slept on the cold floor of the EAU. With blankets provided by the staff, she made a small mattress-like pad on the floor for Kevin. "I don't even know if I was thinking. I was just doing it. When it really hit me [that I was at the EAU] was the next day. I really realized that I would have to stay there, among all of the people and babies and crying. I just freaked out." On the second day, she used a day pass to take Kevin to Nanna's house. "We ran into her apartment, right next door to that nut. I washed up my son and gave him a shower and me a shower and changed his clothes and had something to eat and then we left."

For Denise, the EAU was a difficult experience, one that she is unsure she could do again. "[Kevin] would cry a little bit here and there, [saying], 'I want to go home.' I kept talking to him, 'it's just you and me now. There's nobody else. We got to do this together. We got to work together.' I kept telling him that and encouraging him to please, just bear with me because it's not going to be like this forever. He hung in there with me; I got a trooper." Denise and Kevin spent the next four days shuffling between the EAU, overnight hotels, and Nanna's house before the EAU staff placed them in a transitional family shelter in Harlem. They stayed at the Harlem shelter for four months and when a room opened up at a Manhattan shelter, they were transferred.

A New Start

Denise and Kevin have been living at Manhattan shelter for over seventeen months, and they have been homeless for nearly twenty-two months. While Kevin is in school, Denise attends a training program to become a medical assistant. She has already completed the necessary courses, earning straight A's in her classes, and is currently finishing her internship; she is only one semester away from graduation. Denise's enthusiasm towards school reflects her own motivation for a rewarding career. "I got a seventy-something two times on tests and I freaked out. I thought, 'Oh my God. I don't want it in the seventies!' I wanted all eighties or nineties." This time, she is working hard towards graduation for her own reasons and not for her mother's desires.

While the shelter has become a new type of home for Denise and Kevin, they are eager to move into their own apartment. "I have stuff all packed up. I have this and I had that but I can't get to it because I forgot where I packed it. Since I've been here, I've accumulated so many things. I've been trying to buy little things so when I move I have something. I'm just ready to have my own."

Because of her criminal background, Denise was denied a Section 8 rent subsidy and has been in the shelter system for a longer time than most of the other residents. She is currently appealing the decision and will go to court in the near future. She has already obtained a Certificate of Relief from Civil Disabilities, a certificate granted by the Court to prevent discrimination because of prior criminal convictions. According to a letter of support written by her school counselor, "Denise would be a productive asset to any community. She is responsible, courteous, and has a sincere desire to improve her life and the life of her children." Since moving into the Manhattan shelter, she has participated in their numerous workshops—stress management classes, housing workshops, health classes, and domestic violence workshops.

Denise realizes that her past continues to haunt her and to stall her application's progress in the shelter system. While two years is a long time for her to remain clean, she is very aware that she could easily relapse at any time. She has watched friends fall back into drugs after being clean for two, five, and even ten years. "It could happen [to me], but I'm just praying to God, and I'm trying to do everything that I can possibly do so it won't happen. If I feel like I'm going to turn around and do drugs again, I'm definitely going to call somebody, talk to somebody, scream, yell. I'm going to get somebody's attention. I don't want to go that route anymore. That was a lot of pain for me and I'm tired."

Looking Forward

"I set a goal for forty-five—I'm forty-two now. I want to be married, have a good job, and a nice and safe place to stay for my son. I think that I'm going to get all of those things because I'm working really hard. I've never worked so hard for anything in my life. Before, I didn't have any direction. I was here, there, this, and that. I started everything too young; I always had older friends and I didn't give myself a chance to grow and really experience anything. Now, I feel like I'm a child all over again. I'm looking at the stars at night and stuff like that, and I'm freaking out; I appreciate the little things." Denise is looking forward to having her own apartment, living in her own space, and leading a life without addiction, violence, and fear. "I'm forty-two years old and I've never had my name on a lease. I've had keys but it was just for a room, a rented room here or there, but I've never had a lease. I want to be in my own apartment with my own set of keys so I don't have to worry about knocking on the door, waiting for somebody to let me in the house or them thinking about if they even want to let me in the house. I just want to live in my own apartment for a minute, just to relax and think, 'It's mine, this is finally mine.'"

While Denise is thankful for the many opportunities that a drug-free life has given her in the past few months—independence from Eric, time with Kevin, job training for a sustainable career, and a chance at leading a sober life—she is particularly grateful about renewing relationships with her mother and with Nick. Denise tries to visit her mother every Sunday. They go to church together and Denise says her mother has deepened her spirituality. "I see her every week. Every weekend I'm in Long Island, if I can get there, if I have the money to travel to get there, I'm there every weekend. We have a great relationship."

At fourteen years old, Nick lives with Anthony in Connecticut; he has been separated from his mother for ten years. Denise describes the first time she called Nick. "I was like, 'do you know who this is?' 'No, who?' 'Your mother.' He was like, 'My mother? My mother?' He kept saying that—'my mother? Oh my God, this is my mother?' I was bawling; I was a mess. He was really ecstatic. He dropped the phone and everything. He was just really freaking out. When I finally went to see him, he was crying and I was crying. We just sat down and started talking. I told him—not everything that happened in my life—but I told him what happened: why I left and where I was. He said, 'You know the funny thing about all of that mom? You don't look like you were ever a day on drugs.'"

Although Anthony was briefly married to another woman in the past, Denise is now the only mother figure in Nick's life. Despite his traumatic early childhood, the experience of his father marrying and divorcing, and the knowledge that his mother was living only hours away, drug addicted and floating in-and-out of jail, Nick is a successful high school student, earning straight A's. "He talks to me and says, 'I love you mom,' and it just breaks me. It makes me feel really good and I break down to tears almost every time I talk to him. These days I'm crying because I'm happy and not because I'm sad."

After bringing letters of support from her caseworker, housing specialist, and rehab counselor, Denise won her appeal for a Section 8 housing subsidy. She and Kevin found an eligible apartment and will be moving out within the next few days; they will have spent over two years in the shelter system. During the appeals process, Denise also managed to graduate from her training program and is now a certified medical assistant. She plans to attend a nearby business school to finish additional training and will soon look for employment. She remains drug-free and has no intentions of returning to her previous way of life.

....

National studies estimate that ten to fifteen percent of homeless parents currently have a substance abuse problem, with lifetime prevalence rates ranging from seventy to eighty-five percent.[5] Among New York City families, ten percent (10%) cite drug or alcohol use as the primary reason for their homelessness, and thirty percent (30%) report experiencing substance abuse problems.[6]

Addiction disorders not only lead families to the shelter system, they can also stall a family's progress if the addiction resulted in a criminal record. The typical parent with a history of substance abuse is homeless for eighteen months—ten months longer than the typical parent without a substance abuse history.[7]

NOTES

[1] Emergency Assistance Unit

[2] Although Denise and Anthony never married, they were together for 17 years and some people referred to them as wife and husband.

[3] Denise refers to prostitution as "juggling."

[4] A bench warrant is a warrant issued by a court or judge ordering the apprehension of an offender. It is different from a regular arrest warrant, which is filed by the police rather than the courts.

[5] Ralph da Costa Nunez, *The New Poverty*, Insight Books: New York: 1996: 30.

[6] New York City Commission on the Homeless, *The Way Home: A New Direction in Social Policy*, February 1992: 8, 65, 67.

[7] Institute for Children and Poverty, 2003 Demographic Survey, unpublished.

CHAPTER FIVE
Katherine, age 37

Immigration

People don't come [to the United States] because they have noth-ing else better to do. There's got to be a reason to move your life. I had my challenges—Christy's father—but I came here and I came here to make it; I didn't come here to fail.

Ten years ago, Katherine and her two children left Barbados to escape Richard, the violent and manipulative father of Katherine's youngest child Christy. Keeping Christy virtually captive in his house, Richard had refused to let Katherine see their daughter for extended periods of time. "The man had the child five days out of the week. All I could hear [was] people telling me that the child is screaming and crying...I can't fight it because he would just slap me down. As long as he turns up at the door, I have to hand the baby over to him." At that time, Katherine was nearly a stranger to her seven-month-old daughter, and immigrating to the United States was the only way to protect Christy from Richard's abuse.

Today, Katherine talks freely about her journey from Barbados to the United States; however, remnants of fear and anger occasional-ly remain in her words and harden her stare. Katherine is a small woman with a somewhat frail physique, but her loud voice and strong opinions compensate for any physical lacking. Because of her family's undocumented immigration status, she and her children have lived in the New York City shelter system for nearly four years. Unable to qualify for Section 8 subsidies or public housing, they are stuck in the system. While instability has defined most of her life, living in the shelter system is an entirely different experience. "As a child growing up, you thought of yourself as homeless, in a way, because you didn't have a home that was your own. But it's totally different than this—this is true homelessness."

Conflict from the Beginning

Katherine's childhood was marked by constant transition as she moved from one relative's house to the next. Her mother Margaret overdosed on prescription medication when she was five years old. Even now, Katherine is unsure whether her mother's death was intentional; however, she does know that Margaret was very distraught during the last months of her life. Margaret's mother strongly disapproved of her relationship with Katherine's father Robert. A married man nearly twice Margaret's age, it was widely known that he had numerous mistresses, including women still in their teens. Throughout his life, he would financially support thirteen relationships and would father thirty-six children. Despite feeling jealousy and bitterness about Robert's other lovers, Margaret felt torn between her love for Robert and her familial bond.

When Margaret died, her family and Robert began pointing fingers, each blaming the other for her death. Katherine was caught in the middle of constant quarreling—Robert refused to provide financial support for Margaret's children, and if their grandmother could not afford to raise the children, he planned to send them to an orphanage. "My father wanted to put us in foster care, not a foster home but a big place where you got twenty or forty kids living and sleeping on little beds." Faced with his plan, Katherine's grandmother insisted on raising the three children, but only on a temporary basis because of her constrained financial situation and weakening health.

Although Katherine and her siblings lived with their grandmother for the next eight years, she moved frequently between relatives' houses during her grandmother's financially or physically difficult times. Katherine estimates she lived in seven or eight different homes. "As a child, you don't see it as [being homeless], but you see it as bad because you think you have no place in life. You don't have a mother; you don't have a father. You live with any family member that takes you in for that time."

Living with Robert

Katherine was thirteen years old when her grandmother's already fragile health began deteriorating quickly. Needing a caretaker and wanting to be close to family, Katherine's grandmother decided to visit her youngest daughter, who had immigrated to the United States years earlier. Without their grandmother, Katherine and her two siblings had no place to live and Robert, who was living with one of his many mistresses Martha, decided to temporarily take care of them. Martha was mentally challenged and "could not add five cents to ten cents." Nevertheless, she played surrogate mother to Katherine. "We were happy and Daddy was happy and every weekend—because

Sundays were the only day he would have off—he would take all of us to this restaurant. It was like a KFC but a little bit more detailed and we would go there and go to the beach." For the first time, Katherine felt like part of a stable family.

However, less than a year after moving in with Martha, Katherine and her two siblings again found themselves without a home. Their quiet life fell apart when Martha's teenage daughter discovered she was pregnant. Martha's older sister blamed the unexpected pregnancy on the large household, specifically on Martha's increased parental responsibilities. "Her sister started making waves and she got Martha all upset. She told her, you only got two children from him and now you got five children. You have to deal with five children all of the time—you got to cook for them and wash for them." With her older sister's prodding, Martha and her two children left the house. Katherine and her siblings continued to live with Robert; however this arrangement soon proved difficult. Around this time, Katherine's aunt in the United States offered to raise the children, and although Katherine and her sister decided to stay in Barbados, her younger brother eventually moved to New York City. Katherine spent the next three years bouncing around from house to house, occasionally visiting her aunt and brother in New York.

Despite her lack of stability, she maintained a good-natured attitude and only sporadically resented her situation. "It was only on occasions that I thought [moving around] was a hardship on me, when I thought that I was being used." When Katherine turned seventeen years old, she moved in with her uncle's family, and for the next year, she took care of her uncle's four small children. She cooked them breakfast, helped them get ready for school, and fed them dinner when they came home. Her aunt offered little help, and often stayed in bed until late morning. All the while, Katherine was trying to finish high school, and she felt that the stress caused by her housing situation was directly impacting her ability to keep up with coursework. Although she struggled through her last year of high school, she managed to graduate on time and began working for one of her father's three companies. Still bogged down from housework, Katherine usually arrived at work late and Robert worried that this constant tardiness was setting a bad example for the other workers. After a year of living with her aunt and uncle, she moved back to her father's house.

Unexpected Pregnancy

A year later, Katherine decided that it was time to find her own place, but within a few months of living by herself, she had already moved in with one of her friends, Carlos. Although her feelings for Carlos were not serious, they maintained an intimate relationship over the next three years. "I never thought that I was in love with him and he knew that. We were friends."

At age twenty-three, Katherine discovered she was pregnant with Carlos's child, and she was unsure about her next step. She knew that motherhood would prevent her from working, at least for the first few months, and she would need to depend on somebody. Dissatisfied with Carlos and wanting to not live with him, Katherine felt she had two housing options: her grandmother's house in Barbados or her aunt's place in New York City. Her grandmother, frail and sickly, lived in a small one-room house in Barbados. On the other hand, her aunt Mercedes lived in a three-bedroom brownstone and had the time and financial resources to look after her. After much discussion with her grandmother and her aunt, Katherine decided to temporarily move in with Mercedes. "I came to [the United States] because I was upset that I was pregnant. I needed some place to be and I felt that this was the best place. It wasn't because I wanted to come here to be a citizen; it was just some place to be."

Visiting New York

When Katherine moved to New York City, her younger brother David had already been living with their aunt for nearly ten years, and he seemed less of a brother and more of a distant cousin. While trying to adjust to a new life in New York, she remained uncertain about her relationship with Carlos. Although they were no longer intimate, Carlos was still involved in her life. He traveled to New York in time for her delivery but never signed his name on the birth certificate. The visit was difficult, and Carlos returned to Barbados shortly after their son John's birth. Katherine realized that their previously close friendship had deteriorated into constant bickering; however, she maintained phone contact with Carlos for John's sake. "I never treated [Carlos] badly. He still had access to his son and he could see his son anytime."

The next few months proved difficult—Katherine and her aunt Mercedes fought constantly and Katherine felt almost persecuted by her aunt for the out-of-wedlock birth. At twenty-four years old, she was interested in dating men and attracted the attention of many suitors. However, Mercedes, already upset with Katherine's single motherhood, did not support her dating habits. In her own words, "My aunt is a crumpet, that's my problem; she's a crazy tight-ass."

When John turned three months old, Katherine found a live-in position in New Jersey, working as a caretaker for an elderly woman. It was a twenty-four-hour job: "She needed help to get up and help to go to the bathroom. If she made a mess, you needed to change the bed for her and wash her sheets and wash her clothes, [and] cook all of her meals." The elderly woman's guardians paid Katherine off-the-books and far less than minimum wage for her work. "She wasn't in charge of her own situation. She had money in a trust and those trust-people only cared about her money." Katherine believed that the trustees were taking advantage of her undocumented immigration status by underpaying for her many hours of caretaking. By the end of one year, she was dissatisfied with her low wage and lack of respect.

Around this time, Carlos discovered that Katherine was dating another man, and he was both devastated and infuriated by the very suggestion that this man might raise John; consequently, he moved to the United States. Katherine had heard of Carlos's many girlfriends and was not prepared for his jealously or his spontaneous decision to move to New York. "He came here because he didn't want anybody to be with me while I was raising his son." After nearly a year of infrequent communication, he was suddenly proposing marriage. While Katherine knew neither of them was in love, she seriously considered the proposal for John's benefit. In the end, she decided that marriage would be a poor choice for both of them. "I wasn't comfortable with getting married to him because I didn't think that I was in love. Even though he was talking marriage, I wasn't really talking marriage."

Instead, Katherine and Carlos considered living together. For Katherine, whose own parents were absent from her life, providing John with both a mother and a father figure was very important. "We talked about getting an apartment together and moving in together because we were trying; I was trying." However, the more Katherine stalled in finding an apartment and committing to their relationship, the more upset Carlos became. "The more I was iffy, the more his hate grew, the more the jealously grew. [Eventually], he couldn't talk to me without being angry because of the jealously. He just started to hate me."

Around the same time, Katherine's older sister was visiting from Barbados. With the stress of her relationship with Carlos, the frustration of working for low wages, the difficulty of living undocumented in the United States, and the constant prodding by her sister to move back to Barbados, Katherine decided to leave New York. Barbados seemed to offer more opportunities for financial success and an easy escape from her current dilemma with Carlos. Her sister bought her a one-way ticket and Katherine took John back to their native country. "[My sister] felt that I could go back home and start my own business [in house cleaning]. 'Why stay in this country where you are a foreigner while you could be home in your own country and start your own business and do something?'"

Looking back, Katherine regrets hurrying the decision. "I rushed and went back home. I shouldn't have done it because that wasn't what I wanted to do. I listened to her and it was something that

I regret." Katherine's hasty move temporarily severed all friendly ties with Carlos. Ironically, Carlos, who had originally moved to New York to be with his son, now found himself alone in a foreign country. Although he could have easily moved back to Barbados, Carlos chose to continue living in the United States. Today, Katherine is still sensitive to the pain that she caused him. "I didn't go back to Barbados because I was trying to deny him John. It was just a mistake."

Struggling at Home

Back in Barbados, Katherine and eighteen-month-old John moved in with her sister's family. From the first day, her brother-in-law began making overt sexual advances towards her. "[My sister] had a very unfaithful husband and he would be looking at me and he would say to [his wife], 'she walks about the house not wearing a bra. She is trying to come on to me.'" According to Katherine, her brother-in-law repeatedly asked to sleep with her and routinely spied on her in the house, all the while accusing Katherine of seductive behavior. Relations between Katherine and her sister soon soured and shortly after moving in, she had already started looking for alternate housing arrangements. She soon found herself lacking the emotional and financial support that she was counting on finding in Barbados. "I really thought that [my sister] was going to be there for me. She wasn't. She backed out as soon as I got home."

Katherine found a small, one-bedroom house in a nearby neighborhood and for the next few years, raised John while working as a housecleaner. During this time, she resumed dating, but her brother-in-law was still harassing her. "I used to be terrified of my sister's husband. I couldn't sleep sometimes from just plain fear of that man. To go home at night, I used to have to run to get into my house because I didn't know if he was in the bushes. So many times I would wake up at night and find this man peeping through my window." After a year of stalking, Katherine's brother-in-law was arrested and incarcerated on charges unrelated to the harassment. Years later, she would still have nightmares about the stalking. "Having a window in my room used to scare the daylights out of me because I always felt like he was out there, peeping through the window."

Katherine was still dealing with her brother-in-law's harassment when she started casually seeing Gregory. After a few dates, she was still unsure about her feelings and refused to be intimate with Gregory, but he would not accept rejection. One evening, after a night out, Gregory raped her. At the time, Katherine thought it might have been more of a misunderstanding rather than an intentionally violent act. "The first time, I was just like, ok. I wasn't willing and he was just forceful. I kind of just didn't try to think of it in that kind of way." The next evening, Katherine saw Gregory again, but this time, his intentions were clear and she was raped again. "The second time was more violent and I realized that he really intended to hurt me. It wasn't accidentally hurting me, he really, really wanted to hurt me; it was intentional."

Even after the second incident, Katherine did not go to the police because she had friends in the department and was embarrassed. "I didn't want to say I was raped by my 'boyfriend.' He was my boyfriend and how could your boyfriend rape you? Back then, I didn't know that they had date rape." Katherine tried her best to forget about Gregory and move on. "I didn't want to deal with the issues; I was hurt, I just never went to the doctor. I just left it alone."

Six weeks later, Katherine found out she was pregnant. She decided to tell Gregory about the pregnancy and a few days later, went to his house. "When he found out that I was pregnant, he wanted to rape me. He said, 'the way that I made it in the first place is the way that I'm going to take it out.'" Fortunately, Katherine managed to escape. "I ran away. I was lucky because I ran and I was very scared and I wanted to get a bus or something but God was just good to me. A friend of mine was right there." Even after Gregory's last attempt, she did not press charges.

During this time, Carlos asked Katherine if four-year-old John could visit the United States for the upcoming summer. Still feeling guilty about hurriedly moving back to Barbados and encouraged by renewed communication, she agreed. John stayed with his father for six weeks, but when the time came to return, Carlos refused to send him home. "Carlos kept saying, you're not going back to your mommy; your mommy is coming to you. It would be night and the child would be crying. 'Oh, [your mommy's] going to come tomorrow.' So then John wouldn't cry and would fall asleep. John would get up the next day and he would watch and watch and watch the whole day for me to come and then when night would come and he started to cry and Carlos would go through the same lie again and tell him this lie over and over, every single day. That's what broke the child."

Realizing that Carlos had kidnapped John, Katherine, now nearly five months pregnant, began frantically collecting money in order to fly to the United States to bring John home. However, she had already begun feeling acute, constant pain in her abdomen and difficulties with her pregnancy complicated her plans to rescue John. In the meantime, John's chronic asthma was flaring up and the emotional distress was weakening his physical health. Eventually, Carlos took him to the emergency room. "John was in the hospital and Carlos kept lying that the child was in his care legally. He wrote false letters stating that I had given the child to him, but the doctors kept saying that the child needs to be with the mother."

After nearly five months of living with his father, John returned home. "When he came back to me, he had lost so much weight and had become so thin and so dark, [and] he started having issues: John had never broken one single toy; he started to break toys. John had never been selfish in anything; he came back self-destructive and selfish." Almost immediately after John returned home, Katherine miscarried. John, who had been hoping for a younger brother or sister and was very excited about Katherine's pregnancy, was distraught. "He had gone through all of this [with his father] and then the baby had died and I knew how much it had bothered him, how much it had hurt him."

For all the Wrong Reasons

Within a year of her miscarriage, Katherine became involved with a distant acquaintance, Richard, and soon discovered she was pregnant again. As with Carlos, Katherine's relationship with Richard was not based on love, but rather on a somewhat confused mix of friendship, intimacy, and ulterior motives. "Richard didn't love me.

Getting me pregnant was just to prove that he could." At the same time, Katherine hoped this new pregnancy would help John overcome the trauma he had experienced during the previous year. "I got pregnant really quickly. You usually wouldn't do that but then, you know, the baby dying was hard on John, and I felt that [this baby] would have filled it. That was one of the reasons that I went ahead and had Christy."

Richard was manipulative and violent before Katherine's pregnancy, and his abuse only escalated after the pregnancy caused her to become reliant on his financial support and caretaking. Because of her earlier miscarriage, Katherine's doctor took extra precautions with her pregnancy and she was bedridden for most of her third trimester. Richard occasionally hit Katherine, but most frequently, subjected her to cruel emotional manipulation and abuse. She remembers one incident, in particular. In her third trimester, Christy was breached—her head and feet were not in the correct position for delivery. "We were praying and praying that she would turn, and then the baby started to turn in Richard's presence. She became stuck across my stomach and I was in incredible pain and he was there, laughing at me."

Katherine's doctor, noting that she was under inordinate stress, encouraged her to leave the situation; however, she continued to stay with Richard for reasons that, at the time, seemed rational to her. Katherine was completely dependent on Richard. In addition to monetary support, Richard took care of Katherine and John's daily needs. She told her doctor, "How can I put [Richard] out when he's my only source of support right now and you're telling me that I can't lift nothing heavier than a spoon?" Katherine also pressured herself to stay with Richard because she valued the prospect of marriage and a two-parent household over leaving a violent situation. "I was twenty-seven years old and you start to think that you're getting old and you're never going to get married, and you say to yourself, a lot of other women put up with abuse. Why can't you? You say to yourself, just stick it out." Katherine's focus on marriage also came from her family, which disapproved of her single motherhood. "They had the same idea like me: being too picky."

Escalating Abuse

Katherine gave birth to a healthy baby girl Christy, and within the first few weeks, Richard's abuse had become so unbearable for her that he moved out of the house. While Richard only occasionally resorted to physical abuse, he used the threat of violence to render Katherine submissive to his emotional manipulations. "When Christy was two weeks old, he used to take her for long periods of time and even overnight. Then, from the time that she was eight weeks old, he would have her most of the time and I just used to see her [occasionally]." Under explicit instructions from Richard, his sisters would watch Christy during the day; however, they would often secretly call Katherine: "He's not here and the baby's crying. Come get the little girl."

When Katherine realized that Richard would continue keeping Christy away from her, she was full of regret for not taking earlier action against him. In particular, she felt she should have fled Barbados while still pregnant. "I should have left, I ain't going to lie. I should have left Barbados while I was pregnant. It would have been better for the baby and it would have been better for me, but I was scared to travel on the plane because I had just had a miscarriage."

Instead of quietly lamenting her current situation, Katherine turned to Barbados's child welfare system. When Richard discovered that she had scheduled an appointment to meet with a caseworker, he retaliated by turning the tables on Katherine, reporting her to the same agency for neglect. To her dismay, the caseworker decided to have a roundtable discussion with both of them, instead of a private meeting with only Katherine. "Richard totally dominated the conversation and [the caseworker] heard nothing on my part, which was enough to realize that he probably has hit me before. I left there and I felt really bad. I thought, 'I have to do something for myself. I have to get me and this child away from this man.'"

Escape

After the failed meeting with the caseworker, Katherine decided to take drastic action and planned to secretly take John and Christy to New York City to live with her aunt. Because Richard's name was on Christy's birth certificate, her first battle was getting a passport for her daughter without his knowledge. According to Katherine, the security officers in the passport office kept asking, "What's the story here? Why are you looking for a passport for a seven-month old child? Where's the father?" Responding to the officer's questions, Katherine said, "Listen, this is the situation: I'm in danger, my child's in danger, and I need to get away." After meeting with a number of officials, Christy's application was finally approved.

Once Katherine obtained a passport for Christy, she started

collecting money—working odd jobs and borrowing from friends and relatives—in order to buy plane tickets. During this time, her family still remained friends with Richard, despite his abuse, violence, and near abduction of Christy. Because of this, combined with the fact that news traveled quickly in her small town, Katherine was afraid to tell anyone of her plans for escape. "There was no way that I was going to tell [my family]. If Richard knew at all, I probably could have been beaten to death."

On the day of the planned escape, Richard's sisters, who were taking care of Christy as usual, helped Katherine break into Richard's locked room to obtain important documents pertaining to Christy's birth and identification. "The sisters, they knew what the child was going through; they helped me." When Richard realized that she had taken Christy and John to the United States, he went to the American Embassy in Barbados to try to get them deported. According to Katherine, Richard was unsuccessful because the staff suspected his abuse. "They knew. A woman wasn't going to pick up and do some-thing if there wasn't something wrong."

Today, Katherine's family is still friendly with Richard. They have never sympathized with her abusive situation, which is telling of their views regarding family violence. While she has not heard any recent news about Richard, Katherine does know that he married another woman soon after she fled Barbados. Since leaving, she has never considered returning to Barbados, even during her most diffi-cult times in the United States. "The last few things that happened to me at home were enough for me to never want to go back. You know how people say, oh, I miss home? No, I don't miss home. I don't want to be there. I don't ever want to see home again."

Struggling in New York City

When twenty-eight-year-old Katherine moved to New York City, John was six years old and Christy was almost one. John was a citizen, but Katherine and Christy came to the United States as undocumented immigrants. As planned, her family lived with Mercedes and David for the first few months, trying to adjust to their new life. When Katherine started looking for employment and housing, Mercedes suggested that they continue living with them. Katherine cooked, cleaned, and raised the children. John attended the nearby public school during the day and a neighbor watched John and Christy during the afternoon while Katherine occasionally worked as a housecleaner for private residences.

After nearly four years of living with Mercedes, Katherine was frustrated—personality conflicts and arguments over her love life had become constant and hostile. Moreover, friends and family, both from Barbados and the United States, had begun taking advantage of Mercedes's willingness to accommodate nonpaying boarders, and her large three-bedroom house soon became overcrowded with guests. "Other people started coming to the house and every minute had more than ten people in it. Some might stay a month; some might stay two months; some might stay a little bit longer." Mercedes, a relatively quiet person without a husband or young children, decided that she needed to find a new place, somewhere small and out of the way where guests would not as easily flock. "Mercedes often said, 'everybody knows where I live, everybody knows who I am, and everybody's coming over to me.'" She began looking for a new house, deep in Queens and far from Manhattan and the subway system.

Even without an explicit discussion, Katherine knew she was not invited to move and she started looking for an apartment. Despite their rocky relationship, Katherine was not bitter about the parting. She looked forward to finding her own apartment and gaining a new sense of independence. "I didn't come [to New York City] to depend on Mercedes and that's the truth. I came here with the idea that I was going to get a job, work really hard, get my own place, probably meet somebody nice, and take care of my children and me. I did not think that I would be dependent on her as long as I was."

Moving Out

In part because of her limited finances, Katherine decided to find an apartment with her boyfriend at the time, Nicholas. Katherine quickly found a small apartment—the first and only apartment in her name. Within the first few weeks, Katherine bought new rugs and furniture for the apartment. It seemed that Katherine and her children were on their way to a settled, more independent life. However, within the first month, Nicholas became abusive and Katherine suffered two particularly violent fights before fleeing with her children. "The first time, the stuff was mainly hair pulling and stuff like that, but he [did take] my daughter's carriage and threw it and hit me on my back. The next day was the big fight because I was scared…it's not always the intentions of the person to kill you but it's the unlucky blow that's going to kill. I could have had the unlucky blow the day that he beat me, but fortunately, it wasn't to be."

Katherine did not go to the police and instead, sought refuge at Mercedes's new house. For the next few months, Nicholas lived in Katherine's old apartment, using her furniture and refusing to give back the family's clothing and other belongings. "He kept my children's clothing to perpetuate the abuse. I would have to live through the abuse every single time that I wanted to get anything out of the house." By the time Katherine recovered these belongings, much of the clothing was too small because Nicholas had kept them for so many months.

Meanwhile, Carlos had re-established contact with Katherine. After nearly a decade since their fallout over John's abduction, he was now living in Virginia and dating a new woman, soon to become his fiancé. When Carlos asked to have eleven-year-old John visit during the winter break, Katherine agreed, thinking that he was a different man now. "Carlos took John down to Virginia but he decided that he wasn't going to bring him back." When Katherine realized that Carlos was repeating his previous abduction attempt, she immediately acquired court orders from New York City to bring back John. In February, almost three months after John initially left, Katherine took a bus down to Virginia. "I searched the phone books and called the schools and found out which school he was at. I don't know how Carlos got the child in the school. Red flags should have been going up all over the place. Carlos's name is not even on the birth certificate."

Even today, Katherine has never been able to talk to John about the kidnapping—what happened during those three months or how he feels about his father. "I cannot get any feeling out of John about what happened during that time period. Not then, and not even now, if I ask him." Since the abduction, John has been to therapy and counseling sessions; however, in Katherine's view, he is still unable to deal with the experience. "It's going to come back, eventually. I dealt with it because I had to deal with it and I was an adult, but he was a child. It always comes back when the child gets older."

Another Attempt at Independence

Six months after moving back with Mercedes, Katherine had found another apartment. Her friend, Morris, was renting a house with three bedrooms. A single man in his mid sixties, Morris felt the house was too large for him, and he offered two bedrooms to Katherine and her children. According to Katherine, Morris said that "he had the space and the kids could be there and I could give him whatever I could out of the money I made." Katherine, who was still working as a housecleaner, agreed to pay him half of her monthly income as rent.

After half a year of living together, Morris approached Katherine with an unexpected proposition. "He was interested in…you know, if you're living at my home and you're a girl and I'm a man…[I said], 'well no. It ain't gonna happen.' To have somebody force themselves on you and use you in a situation…I never went there with the idea that was going to happen." The next day, Morris asked Katherine and her children to leave; they temporarily moved back in with Mercedes.

The EAU

Once again, Katherine started looking for a new apartment for her family. At one point, she took six-year-old Christy to the emergency room, the primary place where Christy, as an undocumented immigrant, could go for medical care. One of the nurses noticed that Katherine's address had changed several times over the last few years. The nurse asked what was wrong, and Katherine responded, "I don't have an address to give you right now because it's in the air. The place where I was at, that person asked me to leave." Hospital staff continued to ask Katherine questions and finally, Katherine was given an ultimatum by the hospital's social worker. "She felt like I was not being a good parent and she said, you're going to have to go to the EAU because if you don't, [ACS] is going to have to take the kids away from you." The social worker told her where to go and after picking up a few belongings from her aunt's apartment, thirty-three year old Katherine, twelve-year-old John, and six-year-old Christy arrived at the Emergency Assistance Unit (EAU) in the Bronx. "It was a totally new thing to me. I didn't even know what the EAU was all about."

It took Katherine and her children over a month before their application for admittance into the shelter system was finally approved. During this time, they traveled between temporary hotel placements, staying at each residence only a few days at a time. "We kept being denied over and over again and kept being sent to a different shelter and a different shelter, over and over until we were able to prove that we were truly homeless." Moving around was particularly difficult on John and Christy—each time they moved to a different borough, they entered a new school district. "We did a lot of changing schools but I can't tell you how many schools because we were moving a lot."

Katherine's application for emergency housing was rejected multiple times because EAU investigators believed that the family could continue living with Morris. According to Katherine, Morris denied ever making unwanted sexual advances towards Katherine and told EAU staff that Katherine's family could return to his house. He also denied charging Katherine rent, suggesting that they had a voluntarily intimate relationship. "He lied and everything to make himself look good, but he was making it bad for me." EAU investigators either did not believe Katherine's accusations against Morris or did not care whether they were true. "They were like, 'as long as the house has three bedrooms in it and there's only one person living there, you can go back and live there.'"

In response, Katherine talked to her family's minister and explained her predicament. As soon as she presented a letter from her minister verifying her claims against Morris, her family was approved for emergency shelter. "The letter is what really helped me because I had no proof. You have to prove that you are not lying. Everybody is a liar that goes to the EAU. It's not like you walk into [the EAU] and say you're homeless and get accepted. You have to *prove* that you are really homeless."

An Old Threat

After moving around Manhattan and the Bronx, Katherine and her children were placed in a transitional shelter in Brooklyn. They had lived in the shelter for over a year when Katherine started to suspect that Carlos had found their new residence. She had cut off all contact with Carlos since his second abduction and was terrified that Carlos would make another kidnapping attempt. "He found my aunt's new number since she moved, called her, and asked to talk to John." Although Carlos said he had relocated to Florida, Katherine suspected that he had moved back to New York City. Soon after the phone call, Brooklyn shelter staff alerted Katherine that a man had come to the shelter looking for her. Katherine became anxious. "When I heard that there was this man looking for me, I went to my case manager and said, 'I feel that it's my son's father and if he knows where I am, I don't want to be here.'"

Frightened by the possibility that Carlos had found them, Katherine decided to move her family out-of-state, arbitrarily choosing Ohio. "I packed some of my stuff—only a few things—and I was going to leave everything else. They could throw it away." Katherine, with no family in Ohio and virtually no money in savings, planned to live on the streets with John and Christy. Thanks to the intervention of shelter staff, she eventually abandoned her plans, and instead, her family was transferred to a transitional family shelter in the Bronx.

Today, Katherine says that the idea of seeing Carlos does not frighten her as in the past. She attributes her newfound strength to her experiences in the shelter system—the stress of continually moving around, living with virtually no money, and constantly dealing with other residents, staff, and caseworkers. "After living in a shelter, you had better change—you had better learn to harden up—or you won't survive. You can't live in this kind of environment, with the kind of stress of living inside of this place, without toughening up. I was really soft when I first came into the system, very soft."

Living Undocumented

Living in an unfamiliar area such as the Bronx has been difficult, particularly for Katherine's work. With all of her clients living in
Queens, she has been unable to continue working for those families.
After taking John and Christy to school, Katherine could not get to
Queens in time to spend the hours needed to effectively do her job.
"You're talking about two to three hour bus rides—six hours traveling
just to go and come back. There's very little space in that window to
work." Katherine tried to find new clients in the Bronx but without
a telephone number, arranging appointments was impossible.
Sensitive to negative stereotypes and perceptions of homeless people,
Katherine was very hesitant to give out the shelter's phone number as
her contact information. "[People think I will] steal their stuff—
'Homeless? I'm not going to let her clean my house 'cause she's gonna
clean it for real!'"

Katherine tried contacting domestic worker agencies but very
few places would take her without proper work papers. As an undocumented immigrant, she had few choices. At one point, she did find
one agency that was willing to take her. When she arrived at her first
housecleaning appointment, the man of the house opened the door
without clothes. "They sent me to a guy's house and he was walking
around with his business hanging out and showing me it. [The job]
was supposed to be for sixty dollars for the whole day but I didn't
stay...Agencies that are willing to take you without [documentation],
they think you're willing to do other things to have the job." While

Katherine is very enthusiastic about her plans for working after leaving the shelter system, she seems to have abandoned her hope of working for the immediate time. "I feel uncomfortable trying to set up this kind of business while living in a shelter. No matter who you are, people still have a perception of what you are because you are living in a shelter."

Katherine's inability to find employment has been hard on the family's finances and on her own sense of self-worth. She spends most of the family's public assistance allotment on transportation in order to escort Christy to and from school. In the end, Katherine and her children are left with a little more than $34 each month for the rest of their expenses. "I feel like a bum—a true bum. I never felt this way before. I've been homeless for three years. You realize that you're homeless and jobless—I feel quite retarded."

Despite continually moving around and experiencing instability at home, Katherine's children have managed to do well in school. Christy was accepted to a magnet school for ballet dancing, and John tested into a prestigious Manhattan high school. For his first year, John excelled academically and made honor roll, consistent with his high performance throughout middle school. However, after nearly three years of living in the shelter system, John's grades are now barely passing. "Everybody keeps saying, Katherine, you have to understand. The child's been living in a shelter for over two years, three years by now, and probably the stress is getting to him. But [I say,] 'don't let any stress get to you! Keep your grades up!'" While friends excuse John's slipping grades, she refuses to accept the Ds and Fs that John brings home, and this has become a source of tension and stress within the family.

Katherine and her children have lived at the Bronx shelter for nearly three years, and it has been almost four years since she initially sought help at the EAU. Her applications for a Section 8 subsidy and for an apartment in a housing project have both been rejected due to her family's immigrant status. She has applied for a number of government-subsidized housing units but her family does not qualify because John is the only citizen in their three-person household. According to Katherine, if Christy were also a citizen, her family's search would be easier.

Rejected Again

After nearly four years of living in the shelter system, Katherine's family has received another rejection notice from Section 8 and public housing. Because of a mistake, Katherine's rejection is in Spanish, rather than English, and Katherine views this as a final insult. "They put it in Spanish so I can't even read it!"

At this point, Katherine believes she has no exit from the system. She has spent nearly four of her ten years in the United States living in the shelter system. John has lived his entire adolescence in an institutional setting, sharing one room with his mother and little sister. Christy has lived in the shelter system for almost her entire childhood. When Katherine immigrated here, she never imagined she would continue living "with somebody else over me." Caseworkers and housing specialists have replaced Richard as authority figures, and Katherine feels that she lacks the independent life that a thirty-seven year old mother should have.

Despite the many years living in the shelter system, Katherine remains hopeful and continues to look towards the future. "I do feel a little like my life is in a real slump and I have cried about it, but I want to change that. I would do almost anything to change it—and that's the point. I want to find a way to do this: to be here for my children, to protect my daughter, to raise her, and to do as much as I can for both of my children."

Around her family's four-year anniversary date, Katherine was approved for the Long-Term Stayers Program (LTSP). Within a month and a half, Katherine's family had found an eligible apartment in Brooklyn. After moving out of the Bronx shelter, Katherine returned for one last visit. She gave her caseworker a big hug but intimated that she wanted to leave the past behind her. Katherine has been out of contact since.

....

Almost a fifth of all parents (17%) living in New York City shelters grew up outside of the United States.[1] The majority of these immigrant families are "mixed-status," comprised of any combination of legal immigrants, undocumented immigrants, and naturalized citizens. Nationwide, nearly one in ten families with children (9%) is mixed-status, as are eighty-five percent (85%) of all immigrant families.[2] This shifting nature of immigrant status and complicated family makeup creates confusion in accessing public assistance and can prevent families in need from getting help.

The New York City family shelter system does not turn away people based on their immigration status. However, once families enter the system, they frequently become stuck there, unable to qualify for most government housing subsidies. In response, the Department of Homeless Services (DHS) recently created the Long-Term Stayers Rent Supplement Program (LTSP). Families qualify for the program if they have lived in the system for at least nine consecutive months, have children under age eighteen, receive public assistance, and have been denied Section 8 rent subsidies (or EARP) and public housing. While the program has helped many mixed-status families, undocumented families have again been pushed to the sidelines.

NOTES

[1] Institute for Children and Poverty, 2003 Demographic Survey, unpublished.

[2] Michael E. Fix and Wendy Zimmermann, "All Under One Roof: Mixed-Status Families in an Era of Reform," *Urban Institute.* October 1999.

CONCLUSION

Throughout America, the number of homeless families continues to grow at staggering rates. In response, some people push for the creation of more affordable housing as the way to end homelessness within the decade. Building affordable housing units, expanding the rental subsidy program, and raising the minimum wage to a livable standard are clearly necessary steps in addressing this problem, but they are not the complete answer.

This collection of stories shows how family homelessness is not only about housing, but also about young motherhood, foster care, domestic abuse, addiction disorders, absent fathers, and disengaged mothers. Family homelessness is the story of Rose, a twenty-one year old mother of five, and of Anita, who stayed at over twenty different residences before age twenty-one. It is the story of Lynn, who lived in her apartment for nearly a decade before her abusive husband forced the family to flee, and of Denise, who spent most of her life caught up in drugs, crime, and prostitution before rehabilitation. And finally, it is the story of Katherine, who came to the United States to escape a violent man and start a new life for her family, only to find abusive relationships and exploitative employers. These are the stories of five women, but they reflect the experiences of tens of thousands of homeless mothers throughout this country.

Reading about these women's lives—the misfortunes they faced, the lack of support they received, and the poor choices they made—can be difficult at times. Each suffered from some sort of instability during childhood, whether neglected as a "latch-key" kid like Lynn or moved between foster homes and mental institutions like Anita. As adults, this lack of support and stability only continued, if not increased, and mothers such as Denise and Katherine found themselves without a single friend or family member to turn to for help or understanding.

While these narratives focus on the mothers of homeless families, it is the children who are most affected by the anxiety created by poverty and homelessness. And while this collection of stories describes how a secure childhood is critical for later success, over one million children in the United States are today growing up homeless. What will happen to Anita's daughters Claire and Thalia, who have lived in foster homes for years? How will Katherine's son John, who has spent most of his adolescence in shelters, adjust to living outside the institution's walls; and once outside, will he recover academically? How will Rose's children learn the skills they need as adults when their own mother is still a child herself? With a new generation of children experiencing even greater trauma than that of their parents, the cycle of poverty and homelessness can only continue.

This book was written with the purpose of bringing homeless families—an often hidden problem—into the public eye and to create discussion and dialogue in the hopes of breaking the intergenerational, entrenched cycle of families in poverty. The rising numbers of homeless families in our country have reached emergency proportions and with decreased funding for government services and more restrictions on public benefits, it seems we may have unknowingly replaced the War on Poverty and with a War on the Impoverished.

In his 1995 Vietnam War memoir *In Retrospect,* former Secretary of Defense Robert MacNamara wrote that if only we had asked more questions back then, if only we had looked at more options, if only we had raised the discussion to a higher level, perhaps there would be fewer names on the memorial wall today. The same is true of family homelessness, where the victims are not young soldiers but small children. If we are to effectively address the root causes of homelessness, we must first understand the stories of the *Roses, Anitas, Lynns, Denises,* and *Katherines.* Only by learning from the past and listening to the voices of today can we change the future of family homelessness. Only then can we begin to end homelessness once and for all.

BIBLIOGRAPHY

Burt, Martha R. "What Will It Take To End Homelessness?" *Urban Institute*. October 2001. <http://www.urban.org>.

Fix, Michael E. and Wendy Zimmermann. "All Under One Roof: Mixed-Status Families in an Era of Reform." *Urban Institute*. October 1999.

Institute For Children and Poverty. "Children Having Children: Teen Pregnancy and Homelessness in New York City." April 2003.

---. "Day to Day...Parent to Child: The Future of Violence Among Homeless Children in America." January 1998.

---. "Déjà vu: Family Homelessness in New York City." April 2001.

---. *Homeless in America: A Children's Story.* 1999.

---. "Homelessness: The Foster Care Connection." April 1997.

McLean, Diane E., et al. "Asthma Among Homeless Children." *Archives of Pediatrics and Adolescent Medicine.* March 2004: 158. <http:// www.archpediatrics.com>.

National Campaign to Prevent Teen Pregnancy. "Teen Pregnancy –So What?" February 2004. <http://www.teenpregnancy.org>.

New York City Commission on the Homeless. *The Way Home: A New Direction in Social Policy.* February 1992.

Nunez, Ralph. *A Shelter is Not a Home... Or Is It?* New York: White Tiger Press, 2004.

---. *The New Poverty.* New York City: Insight Books, 1992.

U.S. Conference of Mayors. *Sodexho Hunger and Homelessness Survey 2003.* December 2003.